J. W. De Forest and the Rise of American Gentility

J. W. De Forest and the Rise of American Gentility

James A. Hijiya

Published for Brown University Press by
University Press of New England
Hanover and London

University Press of New England

Brandeis University
Brown University
Clark University
University of Connecticut
Dartmouth College
University of New Hampshire
University of Rhode Island
Tufts University
University of Vermont

Printed in the United States of America
∞

Library of Congress Cataloging in Publication Data

Hijiya, James A.
   J. W. De Forest and the rise of American gentility / James A. Hijiya.
       p.   cm.
   Based on author's thesis (Ph. D.)—Cornell University, 1977.
   Bibliography: p.
   Includes index.
   ISBN 0–87451–454–1
   1. De Forest, John William, 1826–1906. 2. Novelists, American—19th century—Biography. 3. Manners and customs in literature. 4. Social classes in literature. 5. Social ethics in literature. 6. Aristocracy in literature. 7. Democracy in literature. I. Title.
   PS1525.D5Z7   1988
   813′.3—dc19   88–40112
                                                              CIP

5   4   3   2   1

For my mother,
Namiko Hijiya

Contents

Acknowledgments   ix

Introduction: "There is not one single
great man left in America!"   1

1. "He is quite a pretty boy and behaves like
a gentleman."   4

2. "I meant to storm the world's attention."   16

3. "My forte is tittle-tattle concerning living
men."   39

4. "A friend of ours . . . has the craze in his
head that he will some day write a great
American novel."   53

5. "The democratic North means equality—
every man standing on his own legs."   73

6. "His business does not keep him, and so
he works carelessly at it, or he quits it."   94

7. "American freemen hate an aristocrat."   111

8. "Unrecorded he died, perhaps with a bitter
   sense of having failed in life, as has happened
   to many whom earth will never forget."   131

    Epilogue   146

    Notes   149

    References   167

    Index   173

Acknowledgments

This book began as a Ph.D. dissertation ("The De Forests: Three American Lives," Cornell University, 1977) that sketched South American explorer Jesse de Forest (ca. 1576–1624) and many of his descendants, then described in richer detail three of those descendants: the merchant David Curtis De Forest (1774–1825), the novelist John William De Forest (1826–1906), and the inventor Lee de Forest (1873–1961). It was a quaint and deviant dissertation, straying from prosopography, in the direction of the novel; its governing principle was invisible; and no publisher would touch it.

This book is the product of dismemberment. Jesse de Forest and David Curtis De Forest were abbreviated almost out of existence; Lee de Forest was sent looking for refuge between the covers of a separate book; and J. W. De Forest alone escaped. His story, then, is one variation on an old and enduring theme: There is nothing under the sun that is entirely new.

Many people and institutions assisted in the production of this book. Michael Kammen suggested the De Forest family as a dissertation topic, guided the research, criticized the writing, and encouraged me to transform the dissertation into a book. Carol Kammen reminded me that half the family were women, thereby provoking me to discover the papers and person of Harriet Shepard De Forest. Glenn Altschuler, Shaleen Barnes, Michael Colacurcio, Gerard Koot, Clark Larsen, Dick Metcalf,

Betty Mitchell, Larry Moore, Fred Somkin, and John Werly read and criticized various parts of the manuscript in various stages of its development. When I was ready to lay all the De Forests permanently to rest amidst the dust and cobwebs of my attic, Lawrence Levine encouraged me to continue trying to breathe life into J. W.

Many other people assisted in the production of this book. Dorothy Owens of Ithaca College and Cheryl Phillips of Southeastern Massachusetts University typed earlier versions of it. Bonnie Werly provided medical advice. A travel grant from the John Anson Kittredge Educational Foundation enabled me to examine archives around the country.

Perhaps mathematicians owe little to librarians and archivists, but historians cannot say the same. Documents are elusive beasts, and few historians could capture them without the aid of professionals. My thanks, then, to the staffs—both present and long past—of the following institutions: Brown University Libraries, Providence, Rhode Island; Connecticut State Library, Hartford; Cornell University Libraries, Ithaca, New York; Houghton Library, Harvard University, Cambridge, Massachusetts; Manuscripts Division, Library of Congress, Washington, D.C.; the National Archives, Washington, D.C.; New Haven Colony Historical Society, New Haven, Connecticut; Manuscripts and Archives Division, New York Public Library; Genealogy Collection, Rhode Island Historical Society, Providence; Southeastern Massachusetts University Library, North Dartmouth; and Yale University Libraries, New Haven, Connecticut. I owe a special debt to the archivists of the Burton Historical Collection at the Detroit Public Library, who selected and photocopied dozens of hitherto unused documents relating to Harriet Shepard De Forest, then sent me the copies.

If librarians are at one end of the scholarly project, editors are at the other. Ernest Sosa of Brown University Press and Charles Backus and Mary Crittendon of the University Press of New England gently handled a stiff-necked author who was not always convinced of his sin. Professors Lawrence Levine and James Light assisted the editors by evaluating the manuscript and providing constructive suggestions for revision, which often, but not always, were followed. Copy editor Jane McGraw, painstaking and thorough, detected more blunders than I care to admit. It is a custom for authors to absolve their associates of responsibility for any errors in the finished book. For this book, such absolution is not merely customary but practically a matter of moral obligation.

This book is dedicated to my mother, Mrs. Namiko Hijiya. Ever since buying for me the Landmark Book about Genghis Khan and the Mongol Horde, she has encouraged my study of history (and everything else). She plundered her own small resources to help pay for my sojourns in college and graduate school, and she has never hesitated to help me do what I wanted to do. It is fortunate that half the people of this world are unselfish.

South Dartmouth, Massachusetts   J. A. H.
March 1988

J. W. De Forest and the Rise of American Gentility

Introduction

There is not one single great man left in America!

J. W. De Forest, 1852

John Adams and Thomas Jefferson died in 1826. The Revolution was long past, and now its leaders—monuments of a brave old world—were gone as well. A new age now began.

In 1826 J. W. De Forest was born.[1] He would live to the age of eighty and would see many transformations of the world around him—the rise of Jacksonian democracy, the dissolution and reunification of the nation, the abolition of slavery, the coming of industrialization, massive immigration, transcontinental and transoceanic territorial expansion—yet he could not help feeling that he lived in a drab and inconsequential time. Compared to previous generations of Americans—the pioneers of the seventeenth century, the revolutionaries of the eighteenth—those of the nineteenth century seemed small in their accomplishments, ambitions, and ideals. De Forest's father, born in the memorable year 1776, was named John Hancock De Forest; but although he achieved some success as a manufacturer of paper and textiles, he could hardly match the heroic stature of his namesake. To J. W. De Forest it seemed, indeed, that nobody could. After Daniel Webster died in 1852, De Forest lamented that "there is not one single great man left in America!" J. W. De Forest would spend his life wondering what to make of a diminished thing.[2]

In the century of the common man, De Forest believed that America needed extraordinary men. Oh, there were popular idols enough—demagogues like Andrew Jackson, plutocrats like Andrew Carnegie—ambitious men with a genius for gathering dollars or votes. But men of intellect and taste? Men who lived and died for principles? These, De Forest believed, were scarce. The nineteenth century flaunted democracy, and most men interpreted democracy as a general license for the single-minded pursuit of material self-interest (or so it seemed to De Forest). The era was missing both refinement and strength. On the one hand, men were so preoccupied with money that they neglected more elegant articles like literature, art, and manners, not to mention morality and religion. On the other hand, men were going soft—weak, fearful, undisciplined—incapable of making sacrifices or enduring pain. The modern man, as De Forest envisioned him, was a Philistine, but without the elemental vigor of Goliath.

What America needed was gentlemen. As De Forest used the term, a gentleman was a man of uncommon refinement—of good breeding and high ideals—but also a man of strength—of daring and courage and force. De Forest devoted much of his career to studying gentlemen, depicting their virtues, praising their values, and lamenting their absence. His writings contributed to a cult of gentility that flourished in late nineteenth-century America.[3]

De Forest also paid gentlemen the compliment of trying to become one of them. As the son of a self-made businessman, he was embarrassed by his own original lack of refinement. To overcome this deficiency, he fled provincial Connecticut, traveled for years in Europe, and studied the manners and ideas of aristocrats. His relatives were men of business, but he would rise above them as a man of letters. Even as he pursued such sophistication, however, he stumbled into a second embarrassment—the suspicion that he was a weakling. His prolonged travel made him seem useless and spoiled, and his vocation as a writer could be viewed as effete. The more De Forest cultivated the elegant virtues, the more he found it necessary to demonstrate virtues of the rougher sort. Fortunately the Civil War gave him his chance. By serving in the Union army, he showed that he could write *and* fight. When he died in 1906, his gravestone would feature a pen crossed by a sword—emblem of the complete gentleman. If America lacked heroes, it was not the fault of J. W. De Forest.

This is not to say that De Forest's devotion to gentility was perfectly uniform throughout his long life. Although he always admired gentlemen, that admiration reached different levels of intensity during different periods of the nineteenth century. De Forest's intellectual biography may be divided into three phases that correspond (very roughly) to three political movements: the Whig (1826–1860), the Republican (1861–1868), and the Mugwump (1869–1906). During his Whig phase, De Forest acquired a balanced set of aristocratic and democratic prejudices. He learned to view the general run of people as coarse, small-minded, and selfish; but he also learned to view them as sensible, industrious, and good-hearted. He could ridicule the vulgarity of the American people but, at the same time, applaud them as the most virtuous people on earth. During De Forest's second (and briefest) phase, the Republican, his balance of aristocratic and democratic values shifted in the direction of the latter. As De Forest took up arms in a war that vindicated free labor and abolished slavery, he made human equality an ideal. Although he continued to disdain "boors" and to honor the "reputable classes," he now perceived himself and his country as champions of the "plain people." It was during this Republican phase that De Forest produced the writings by which he is best remembered, most notably the novel *Miss Ravenel's Conversion*. After 1869 De Forest rapidly and permanently lost faith in democracy and assumed an attitude even more aristocratic than that of his Whig phase. Although the term *Mugwump* was not in common usage before 1884, it could be applied to De Forest in the 1870s, when he had become disillusioned with the masses of Americans and disaffected from his country and his times. He spent the next three decades deploring the "low-born rabble of Philistines"; defending the privileges of well-to-do male Anglo-Saxons; and, with only occasional misgivings, elevating the gentleman almost to the status of a god. It was during this long, last phase of his life that De Forest reached the apotheosis of gentility.

Chapter 1

He is quite a pretty boy and behaves
like a gentleman.

John Hancock De Forest, 1826

J. W. De Forest was an American of old stock. When he was born, his family had been in the New World for two centuries. In 1623 Jesse de Forest, a Walloon who had lived in Avesnes and Leiden, led an expedition to found a colony in what is now Guiana. Although Jesse died in 1624 and his settlement was abandoned, he may have inspired those Walloons who, in that same year, started to people a northern colony that would eventually become New York. Two of his children settled in that colony in 1637, and in about 1694, his grandson David moved to Connecticut, establishing there the best-known branch of the family tree. One of Jesse's great-great-great-great-grandsons was born in Humphreysville, Connecticut, and was christened John William De Forest.[1]

Old family does not necessarily mean old money. In view of J. W. De Forest's preoccupation with gentility, it is noteworthy that he was the son of a self-made man. John Hancock De Forest, the novelist's father, made a slow, unsteady, and uncertain climb to economic and social respectability. He was born on a farm in Connecticut, invested his small inheritance in a store in Maine, went bankrupt, worked as a clerk and supercargo (commercial agent on a ship), again went into business for himself, prospered for several years as a merchant and broker in Connecticut and New York, but by 1821 was losing so heavily that he was ready for what his brother David Curtis De Forest called a "dernier resort." Disgusted with commerce, John sank all his remaining capital into a new enterprise, manufacturing. Going into partnership with two Philadelphians, he purchased the disused millworks at Humphreysville (later renamed Seymour), Connecticut. As president of the Humphreysville Manufacturing Company, he set the paper-, grist-, and sawmills going and converted the woolen mill to the production of cotton sheeting. In this industrial undertaking, the forty-four-year-old neophyte was supported by his brother David, who had made a small fortune in Buenos Aires as a merchant and a sponsor of privateers. David lent John more than $8,000—half of John's investment in the mills—and the enterprise proved profitable. By 1827 John could repay the loan in full (to David's widow), and for the rest of his life he lived in comfort. Becoming a respected man in Humphreysville, he served as a judge and state legislator.[2]

While building his fortune, John Hancock De Forest also produced a family. In 1811 he married Dotha Woodward of Watertown, Connecticut, whose ancestors had come to America at about the same time as his own, and the union resulted in four offspring who reached adulthood. George Frederick was born in 1812, Henry Alfred, in 1814, Andrew Woodward, in 1817, John William, in 1826. Among the two parents and four children there were certain common characteristics—a family resemblance—but there were also some important differences that help explain certain complications in J. W. De Forest's character.[3]

In religion, for example, the father and the mother represented the opposing poles of reason and piety. To be sure, John Hancock De Forest was a religious man: the first article of his will, made out in 1837, dispensed of his soul and body "to the beneficent providence, and the tender and forgiving grace and mercy of Almighty God." Still, although an undoubted and undoubting believer, De Forest displayed rational broad-mindedness. Though he read the Bible, he also read the Koran. In his letters to his sons he spoke rarely of God and never of Jesus. His lack of commitment worried his brother Ezra, a more fervent Christian, and prompted Ezra to ask him whether it was "safe postponing repentance toward God & faith in our Lord Jesus Christ until a more convenient season." Meanwhile, as John Hancock De Forest awaited a more convenient season, it fell to Dotha Woodward De Forest to educate the children in the faith. She repeatedly begged them to "embrace the Saviour" and hoped they would all enter "the kingdom of Christ." During the height of the Second Great Awakening, she rejoiced to see "the Spirit of the Lord" at work in the "interesting revivals." Dotha De Forest's religion provided her with a moral earnestness her husband lacked. It was only her "urgent suit" that put an end to his practice of offering wine and spirits to thirsty guests.[4]

The difference between the father and the mother appears in the letters they wrote to George and Henry, who were away at school, after the death of an infant son in the winter of 1825–1826. John Hancock reported the parents' "perfect assurance" that God would take the child "to Heaven, where he would be always happy." Dotha agreed, saying, "the dear little child has gone we believe to a better world," but then she added this: "and we are left to prepare to follow him, you are old enough now my dear children to think of these important things, and I hope you will not suffer yourselves to close your eyes to sleep one night, without first remembering your duty to God." Whereas the father never bothered his children with "these important things," the mother never missed an opportunity to do so.[5]

With the assistance of a wave of revivalism in the 1830s, Dotha inculcated Christian piety in her children. In 1837 Henry reported from Rochester, New York, where he was beginning a medical practice, that the evangelist Charles Grandison Finney had done a "good work" there. Four years later, Henry demonstrated his own religious commitment by going to Syria as a medical missionary for the American Board of Commissioners for Foreign Missions. He stayed there thirteen years. Meanwhile, Andrew aimed at "complete purity of heart & not less at holiness of conduct," filled his diary with meditations, and prayed that the "all prevailing spirit" of God would move upon "cold hearts." He and George both became superintendents of Congregational Sunday schools. The De Forests lived as Christians and died the same way. When George lay on his deathbed in 1882, he displayed "christian fortitude and cheerfulness" and (if newspaper accounts can be believed) expressed his highest values with his last words: "Mother—Heaven."[6]

It is said that when J. W. De Forest died, he too "never faltered in his religious faith," a faith he had acquired early. Reared in a family of Sunday school teachers and missionaries, he was bound to contract the divine contagion. When he was twenty, his sister-in-law compared him to Richard Baxter, the seventeenth-century, English Nonconformist. De Forest was, she reported, "one of the most truly godly men I have ever known & reminds me of what I suppose Baxter & those old worthies to have been." Even as a young man, De Forest seemed like a Puritan.[7]

Along with religion, the De Forest boys imbibed a demanding code of morality. In 1836 and 1837, all four signed a pledge of abstinence from liquor; later, Andrew would take an active role in temperance reform, and J. W. would inject his novels with small sermons on the evils of drink. Helping their mother keep the family morally straight, the boys exhorted each other to stay on the path of virtue. When Andrew moved to the city that his mother called "Sodom" and that other people called New York, George suggested that he avoid the theaters, and Henry urged him to attend church regularly. Thus their mother's evangelism defeated their father's indifference, at least for a while.[8]

While Dotha De Forest was teaching her sons to be Christians, John Hancock De Forest was teaching them to be businessmen. As a self-made businessman, he inculcated in his sons the tried-and-true mercantile virtues of diligence, economy, punctuality, and prudence. When twelve-year-old Andrew went away to school, the father urged him to "exert all your powers to learn what you can between this time and vacation. Improve every minute." De Forest urged George and Henry to use money with "prudence and discretion" and advised them to keep account books. He was "mortified" when he discovered that one of his young cousins was acting "like a fop and a bean, instead of a student," spending his father's hard-earned money on "fooleries." Planning to make a merchant of his own son Henry and a lawyer of son George, De Forest told them that "I want all my boys to be well fitted for men of business." When, on one occasion, the sons failed to answer letters promptly, he reprimanded them as strongly as he knew how: "This is not like a man of business."[9]

Despite this businesslike attitude, however, John Hancock De Forest was by no means a Philistine. When not occupied with the manufacture of lumber or cloth, he busied himself with the study of books. His library included Xenophon, Plutarch, Shakespeare, Cervantes, Bunyan, Milton, Dryden, Pope, Cowper, Hume, Gibbon, Franklin, and Hamilton; and it was said that his greatest pleasure was reading, especially in the English classics. Valuing a liberal education, he encouraged his sons to do well in school by buying them presents as rewards for "first rate scholarship." He told them he expected that "the De Forest youths will go ahead of every body" at school and that they would conduct themselves "with so much propriety, and study so well, as to do honour and credit to your name and family." Thus he taught them not only to be businesslike but also to be scholarly. He taught them, that is, to be gentlemen.[10]

John Hancock De Forest had not been able to attend college, but he sent his first two sons to Yale. George was one of a handful from the class of 1831 who became merchants or manufacturers instead of ministers or lawyers; Henry, class of 1832, became a physician. Both sons shared their father's gentlemanly ideals. When Henry moved to Bristol, Connecticut, in 1835, he told George that the people in the clock-making capital of America lacked the ideas, the information, the ability to converse on general topics that were common in Humphreysville. Though shrewd and pious, the men of Bristol had no "poetry" in them: "the truth is," said Henry, "they have *learned* but little except what bears upon the making of clocks." Well-bred men like the De Forests could look with disdain upon the boorish manufacturers of Bristol.[11]

The genteel aspirations of the family were clearly, almost painfully, exhibited by Andrew De Forest. Apparently the least bookish of the sons, he entered business at the age of fifteen and never bothered going to college. He began by clerking in a store, worked his way up to being a partner in a lumber company, and ended up as a bank director and the president of the New Haven Gas Light Company. He was a busy man who found it difficult to take time out for reading: "The pocket," he said, "is constantly whispering—this will never do." Nevertheless, Andrew De Forest *did* read: not only the Bible and John Bunyan, but also Sophocles, Pliny the Younger, Bacon, William Robertson, Taine, Macauley, Scott, Cooper, and Hawthorne. Andrew valued education so highly that he even forced himself to read books that he disliked. In 1847 he was bored by a volume of Thomas Arnold's historical lectures but continued reading them "for the exercise" anyway, because he believed that "business does not discipline the mind much & nothing but study will." For a De Forest, disciplining the mind was just as necessary as filling the pocket—even if it meant suffering through the tedium of lectures on history.[12]

Striving to be gentlemen, the De Forests always considered themselves members of an elite. David Curtis De Forest, for example, never doubted that he was one of "the virtuous few" who belonged to "the civilized & well bred portion of mankind." His nephew John William learned early to look down upon "chambermaids & the like of that," and in old age he would be proud of the fact that his family "belonged to the classes rather than to the masses." Henry objected to the way in which Southerners "lay claim to all the generosity & all the 'chivalry' in the nation . . . while the Yankee is a mere money making machine"; as a chivalrous New Englander, he resented the cavaliers' exclusive claims. Although the De Forests were businessmen, they never were *only* that.[13]

Like many other Americans who made an ideal of gentility, the De Forests voted Whig. They congratulated each other in 1834 and again in 1838 on the defeat (locally) of Jacksonians, and Andrew fretted in 1840 that the Democrats sought to overthrow the Constitution through the enlargement of presidential authority and patronage. John William made heroes of Whig leaders Daniel Webster and Henry Clay; and after they died, he worried that "a new race of statesmen has now succeeded to power among us,—the men of 'progress,' the annexationists,—the demagogues." He believed that the Whig Party represented the intelligent and principled elite, while the Democratic Party represented the undistinguished but efficiently organized multitude. When an old acquaintance, a man "never considered anything uncommon," was elected to Congress as a Democrat, De Forest concluded that "it was a repetition of the old story of Polk & Pierce: a middling man taken because nobody had anything in particular to say against him, & then elected by the peculiar party-cohesion of the Democracy." The De Forests, like other Whigs, prided themselves on valuing principle above party, and the outstanding individual above the masses.[14]

Not that the De Forests despised democracy. Contemporaries of Jackson and Lincoln, they too perceived value in the common people and justice in popular rule. When J. W. read Eugene Sue's novel *The Mysteries of Paris,* he said that its "greatest recommendation" was its "democratic tendency, being written to shew the sufferings which the people have in all ages suffered from the hands of the great"—hardly the judgment of a champion of aristocracy. Moreover, even though the De Forests admired the American elite, they considered membership in that group to depend not on birth, as in an aristocratic society, but on achievement, as in a democracy. Though David counted himself among the "virtuous few," he also acknowledged his "humble birth." The upper class was not restricted to certain lineages but was permeated by talented people who had come up from the classes below.[15]

The democratic temper of the De Forests' elitism was illustrated by the fact that they did not call themselves aristocrats, but gentlemen. The word *aristocrat* connoted the feudal past, arbitrary privilege, the suffering of the people from the hands of the great. But *gentleman,* while serving the purpose of social discrimination, had a less noxious connotation. The De Forests would accept the definition offered some years later by William Dean Howells, who said that a gentleman was not "a person born to wealth or station, but any man who has trained himself in morals or religion, in letters and in the world."[16] In the ages of

Jackson and Lincoln, the De Forests adhered to the ideal of the self-made gentleman. It would not be until the ages of Grant and McKinley that J. W. De Forest would discard that ideal.

If the De Forests' devotion to business was moderated by their aspiration to gentility, it was affected in two somewhat contradictory ways by their religion. On the one hand, religion stimulated them to great economic exertions: they believed that hard work provided not only physical but also spiritual well-being. As Andrew said in 1840, "A man is under contract to make the best use of his talents—to employ them for the good of mankind & as an ultimate end—the glory of God." Besides saying that wasting time was a dereliction of Christian stewardship, Andrew warned that when one's mind was not "imperatively occupied," one was subject to "wandering thoughts" and "reveries" that lured one into sin. Therefore, for God's sake as well as Mammon's, one was duty-bound to labor. On the other hand, the De Forests' religion prevented them from equating virtue with the acquisition of shekels. At the same time that Andrew identified "wandering thoughts" as one of the "approaches of Satan," he also identified "the business of the world" as another. Henry, similarly, welcomed religious revivals because they counteracted "the influence of political excitement, devotion to business, & a spirit of speculation." While religion inspired the De Forests to work hard, it did not necessarily inspire them to work for wealth. George and Andrew were businessmen; but Henry was a missionary, and J. W. was a novelist. Thus, religion joined gentility as a force resisting mere acquisitiveness, and the De Forests had to reconcile three partially conflicting roles: businessman, gentleman, and Christian.[17]

It was into this complicated family that a child was born on March 31, 1826. "A very pretty baby," the newcomer was at first called simply Tom Thumb, but within a few months he inherited the name of an infant boy, John William, who had died the previous winter. From the beginning, J. W. De Forest's life was shaped by illness, suffering, and the proximity of death.[18]

Neither of his parents was robust. His father was a slender man with rheumatism and "weak lungs"; his mother endured chronic indigestion and "extreme irritability of nerves." When pregnant with the second John William, Dotha contracted a bad case of influenza (which may account for the child's weak constitution). When the boy was three years old, his mother's hands trembled so badly she could scarcely write, and for months at a time she could not go to meeting. In 1839 John Hancock De Forest reported that his wife was "not well, tho nearly as well as usual."[19]

With such sickly parents, the children could hardly be expected to be paragons of health. Of eight offspring, four died in infancy or childhood. Of the survivors, George and Henry seem to have been healthy during youth, but Andrew suffered from severe nosebleeds and crippling rheumatism. Frailest of them all, however, was John William, who endured chronic bronchitis from at least his eighth year onward. At age twelve he was stricken with typhoid fever, and seldom thereafter did he enjoy prolonged good health.[20]

The De Forest youths responded to the omnipresence of sickness and death by discovering the redemptive power of pain. Rather than simply lament their suffering, they interpreted it as a chastening rod that spurred them to moral improvement. Believing that life was "a vale of doubts & fears," Henry told George that "I expect trouble & disappointment here & I really believe that it is best I should have it—it would work for my good." Not long after Henry hoped for this salutary malady, Andrew actually endured one. In 1839 Andrew suffered an attack of rheumatism that confined him to bed for three months, and shortly thereafter he observed that the dispensations of Providence had made him a better man. "It is hard to improve," he said, "while the current of prosperity fills every hope & gratifies almost every desire, but when disease or misfortune meddle with life, then is the favored moment for it to renew itself, to rise and take a long stretch in improvement."[21] Reared in a family that saw torment as potentially beneficial, J. W. De Forest would in later years interpret the Civil War as a splendid agony that restored moral vigor to a decadent America.

Because of his mother's debility, "Master John" spent the first year of his life with relatives in nearby Woodbridge, Connecticut. His father visited him there frequently, and occasionally the child was brought home for a day or two. John Hancock De Forest watched his son's growth with good-humored pride. In September 1826 he told George and Henry that the five-month old was universally acknowledged the brightest lad in Woodbridge, and in November he reported that "he is quite a pretty boy and behaves like a gentleman." The infant son was taken to meeting each Sunday when the weather was good, and once he laughed out loud during a sermon. "I suppose," said the father, "he did not like the preaching."[22]

In April 1827 the child came back to Humphreysville, where he spent most of the next two decades. At age three he was "a very good boy" except that, for some reason, he resisted learning to read. In March 1833 the future pioneer of literary realism observed that the first day of spring looked much like winter. John began attending a "select school" in 1836—apparently his first taste of formal education. In February 1837 he wrote his first letter, one to Henry, who was trying to establish a medical practice in Rochester. In this note John reported that their father intended to swear off tobacco on April 1. "I don't think he will be an April fool," said the ten-year old, "but rather the reverse." The boy was a competent and confident writer. Later in 1837, when asked by his teacher to produce a composition on a subject of his choice, he wrote an essay on "the manners, customs, and habits of the American Indians." When called upon to read their compositions at an "exhibition" (presumably for the parents of the scholars), some of the students found it embarrassing. "But for my part," John told his brother Andrew, "I got along very well, and was much amused."[23]

In February 1839, when John was twelve, his father died suddenly of a "bilious fever." Though well-to-do, John Hancock De Forest had lost heavily during the depression of 1836–1837, when his mills had been "worse than unprofitable," and his estate at the time of his death was valued at only $31,000, of which $21,000 was in the stock of the Humphreysville Manufacturing Company. His will divided the property evenly among his wife and children, and George De Forest took over the direction of the factories. During the next six years, however, the company did not prosper, and in 1845 the family sold all their shares for a total of $17,000. From this transaction, John received almost $3,000—plus perhaps a keen sense of unstable fortunes, a sense that later would shape fictions of social climbers and of genteel families in decline. In 1846 J. W. De Forest invested in a paper mill in Humphreysville, and probably at about this time he became a silent partner in brother Andrew's lumber business in New Haven.[24]

Bad health apparently deterred John from following George and Henry to Yale. In 1846 he headed for the Middle East instead, in the hope that a sea voyage and a change in climate would ease his bronchial condition. Four years earlier, brother Henry had gone to Lebanon (then part of Syria) as a medical missionary, and John now went to visit him there. He arrived in Beirut in about March of 1846, then joined his brother at Bhamdun, a town in the highlands a few miles southeast of Beirut. While Henry, his wife, Catharine, and other missionaries labored to free Syrians from what Catharine called "their dead forms of religion," John tried to regain his health. On Henry's professional medical advice, he inhaled tobacco smoke through an *argeeleh* (a kind of water pipe)—a remedy, he said, that soothed his throat better than any other medicine. By July he was telling his mother that he hoped to be cured, or at least relieved.[25]

Meanwhile he explored the Holy Land: Beirut, Jerusalem, Damascus, the smaller towns, and the countryside. To his dismay, he found that religion there, both Moslem and Orthodox Christian, exalted the ridiculous: "pilgrimages, shrines, and the like stupidities." He described the bathing of pilgrims in the Jordan as a "washing of the dirtiest of possible sheep in the dirtiest of possible rivers" and called it "one of the strangest pictures that ever superstition mosaicked out of morsels of stupid humanity."

The sacred places and practices of Jerusalem, said the skeptical Yankee, excited "unbelief and irreverence rather than faith and devotion."[26]

In the travel book that he published nine years after leaving Syria, he did not conceal his disdain for the beliefs, customs, and people of that land. He told approvingly, for instance, of how an American provoked glares by strolling at the base of a wall holy to Moslems, although he had been ordered away. "Our customs permit me to walk anywhere that I can," the American told the "speechless" natives, and De Forest interpreted the event by saying, "The American eagle soars in the face of the sun, and is not to be cowed by the horsetails of a dilapidated crescent." As for the Syrian people, De Forest found them inquisitive and sociable, but envious, deceitful, vain, and lacking in "moral courage."[27]

Early in February 1847 De Forest left Syria, and he probably was back in Humphreysville by the time his mother died. Dotha Woodward De Forest, after many years of poor health, gave up the ghost on October 15, 1847. Like her husband, she divided her estate evenly among her survivors, with each of the four sons receiving property worth about $3,700. In 1849 John, perhaps making use of this inheritance, purchased real estate in Derby, Connecticut, and he may also have invested further in his brother Andrew's lumber business. But although he had reached his majority, J. W. De Forest was not yet ready to undertake gainful employment. Leaving his fiscal affairs in Andrew's hands, he began writing a history of the Indians of Connecticut.[28]

Chapter 2

I meant to storm the world's attention.

J. W. De Forest, *Seacliff*, 1859

Though remembered mainly as a novelist of the Civil War, J. W. De Forest was an established writer well before the firing on Fort Sumter. His *History of the Indians of Connecticut* came out in 1851, when he was only twenty-five years old, followed by the travel book *Oriental Acquaintance* in 1856, the serialized novel *Witching Times* in 1856–1857, the travel book *European Acquaintance* in 1858, and the novel *Seacliff* in 1859. In addition, beginning in 1855, he published book reviews, articles, and short stories. In these works, he began discoursing on the themes that would engage him for the rest of his life: the present and the past, reality and romance, the quotidian and the sublime, the common man and the gentleman. (These themes will be analyzed in chapter 3.)

He did not plunge recklessly into the writing profession. Instead, he eased into it with the gingerliness of a man entering a very hot bath. He told his family that he did not want to be an author; so profound was the denial, that he repeated it in the preface to his very first book. He was particularly slow to begin the dubious business of novel writing. His first book was a history, his second, a narrative of travel. Before he published a work of fiction, he spent a decade wandering in the Middle East, Europe, and the American South, as if to elude his calling for as long as possible.

J. W. De Forest's career as a writer began with the Indians of Connecticut. Ever since childhood he had been interested in

America's original inhabitants, having composed a school theme on the subject as early as 1837. In Humphreysville he had seen a few surviving but degenerate specimens of the race, whom he remembered as "coarse and stupid" and "bloated with liquor." Nor was he the only member of the family fascinated with the natives. In 1840 and again in 1841, Andrew jotted in his diary brief histories of the Indians of Humphreysville. As the aborigines seemed about to vanish from the land, their successors tried to preserve a memory.[1]

Beginning probably in early 1848, John toiled single-mindedly on the history. Traveling on horseback because doctors said the open air would be good for him, he explored libraries in more than a dozen small towns, in addition to the Yale College library, the state archives in Hartford, and the collections of the Massachusetts and Rhode Island historical societies. By January 1850 he had completed the manuscript, and, after getting a prefatory testimonial from the Connecticut Historical Society, he published his first book in 1851.[2]

At the time of its publication, as well as more than a century later, the history was praised for its fair treatment of Indians. In 1851 a New Yorker, planning to publish a weekly paper dedicated to the claims of the Native Americans, asked De Forest to contribute articles to the journal, saying that no one could more justly be called "the friend of the Red Man." In 1964, in his introduction to the fifth edition of *History of the Indians,* Wilcomb E. Washburn said that De Forest, "a remarkably detached observer and shrewd analyst," repeatedly demonstrated "an ability to understand the Indian point of view and to sympathize with it." Unlike some previous historians, De Forest did not portray Europeans as thoroughly virtuous; rather, he scrupulously recorded what he called "the unjust and relentless policy of the colonists" and presented the Indians' view of such events as the Pequot War and land cessions.[3]

Nevertheless, there is some doubt that he merited the epithet "the friend of the Red Man." Throughout the history, De Forest depicted Indians as perfect savages: fanatics who worshipped the devil, roasted their own children in sacrificial fires, and learned "to love war, to love revenge, to lay no restraint upon the indulgence of their passions." As a civilized man, De Forest shuddered when he thought what America would have been without European improvement:

> Tracks of wild beasts would be found, where now extends the solid pavement, trodden by thousands of human feet; the savage bear would be seen coming out of his hollow tree, where now crowds of intelligent youth are emerging from the seats of learning; the screams of the wild cat, or the panther, would be heard where now resounds the busy hum of machinery, or the sweet melody of sacred music; the land, which is now as the garden of Eden, would then be a desolate wilderness.[4]

Determined to see the wilderness made into a garden, De Forest could not tolerate wild beasts, whether on four legs or two.

Moreover, although he deplored the Europeans' cheating and murdering of Indians, he refused to blame the Europeans for the Indians' demise. Maintaining that the native population before white contact was much smaller than previously estimated and was not growing, he asserted that disease and demoralization, not the policies of the whites, were the true causes of extermination. Whenever civilized people met "barbarians," the latter were bound to fade away. Even if the Indians had never suffered violence or fraud, they would have perished nearly as quickly. "Their own barbarism," said De Forest, "has destroyed them." Like John Gorham Palfrey and other nineteenth-century historians, De Forest asserted that the triumph of "progress" over "savagery" was inevitable. Thus, although the Europeans had not lived up to their Christian and civilized precepts, they had not been guilty of "any particular degree of heedlessness, or inhumanity, or injustice." The Indians had not been destroyed by whites, but by the Indians' own physical and moral weakness.[5]

When John De Forest began researching his history of the Indians, he was twenty-two years old, he had never held a job, and he had decided upon a vocation to which he would not admit in public. "I always had an ambition to be an author," he recalled in old age, "even when I was a little boy." By the time he was a teenager, he said, he had decided to be a novelist, and he produced his history of the Indians "for the practice of writing." In 1850, when De Forest sent his manuscript to the Connecticut Historical Society for endorsement, he did so because he thought the "imprimatur" would promote sales. "I am determined," he told the society, "to *print* anywhere." Thus, early in the going, he deliberately pursued a writing career.[6]

History of the Indians of Connecticut, however, began with a disclaimer. "It was no intention of becoming an author," averred the author, "but a real love of the subject, which first led me to pay attention to the story of the aborigines of Connecticut."[7] Early in his career, De Forest denied or played down his literary aspirations, and throughout his life he felt uneasy in his calling. In part this uneasiness was due to pressure from his relatives, but in large measure his equivocation stemmed from doubts of his own.

One cause of his discomfort with the pen was the fear of appearing presumptuous. It was not easy to write well; it was not easy to make a living as a writer; to do both was practically impossible. As J. W. De Forest forsook ordinary business and entered upon a profession in which the chances of success were outrageously slight, he tried not to make his plans known to his acquaintances, dreading what he called their "troublesome questions & tiresome jokes." A correspondence with his brother Andrew in the summer of 1848 illustrates this desire to conceal extraordinary ambitions. Regarding the younger brother's work on the history of the Indians, Andrew jabbed a raw nerve when he told him, "You have undertaken a work which, if success is not equal to your present anticipations will do you good in more ways than one." When he read this, John interpreted it to mean that failure at writing would force him to pursue more attainable goals. Resenting this "slur on my jugement [sic]," he denied that he "was carried away by a fancy for being something out of the ordinary." Originally, he said, he had not intended to spend much time or effort on the Indians; only after months of study had he realized how large the project had to be. The point was that he had not begun his work with "presumptuous notions." Moreover, he said, he had not yet even come to "the desperate resolution of publishing"; if his throat should heal enough so that he could enter "active life," he might give up the history entirely.[8]

The rarity of literary success gave De Forest a second misgiving about becoming an author: he feared that writing would not bring home much bacon. In a letter to Andrew in 1852, he called the pen "a poor thing to live by," and in his subsequent fictions, he said repeatedly that a man should take up writing only after being assured of income from some other source. "The pen," he said, "is an uncertain means of existence," and "no man should voluntarily place himself in the condition of living from hand to mouth." As the son of a prosperous businessman, De Forest had grown accustomed to comfort, and he did not intend to undertake the romantic role of the starving artist.[9]

Accompanying this financial consideration, however, was a third and more fundamental one: it was hard to take writing seriously. In the nineteenth century (as in some other times), the business of America was business, and literature was viewed by many as the pointless pastime of useless people. Popular writers like Nathaniel Willis and Ik Marvel deprecated their work by calling it trifling; only unpopular writers like Henry James insisted that novels mattered. Washington Irving wrote a story in which a poet wisely renounced his "cursed, sneaking housekeeping employment, the bane of all true manhood." Literature became increasingly the property of the idle and unproductive—the property, that is, of middle-class women. Most books were bought and read by women; most were written by women, or by men of suspiciously tender sensibilities. In such an environment, any self-respecting man would think twice before joining what Nathaniel Hawthorne called a "damned mob of scribbling women."[10]

J. W. De Forest thought twice, and then some. Despite his desire to write, he would always harbor prejudices in favor of a more "active life." In later years, he would satirize academics, describing one of them as "thin, pale and almost sallow . . . fragile . . . dreadfully ladylike"; and he would despise "that Yankeehood which stays in corners, speechless and impotent—a community of old maids, toothless doctors, small-souled lawyers, village poets, and shrivelled professors." Always honoring men who bustled in the world, he would eventually go so far as to say that "the man who best manages his fellow men—the great general or the great statesman—is the leading man in the world in regard to ability." The great writer, alas, was not so "able." J. W. De Forest would never be entirely convinced that writing was suitable work for a man.[11]

Early in 1850, with his history of the Indians nearly ready for publication, De Forest sailed to Europe, where he spent the next four or five years traveling, observing, and writing. Drawing income from his investment in Andrew's lumber company, this son of a businessman lived the carefree, idle life of a born gentleman. Occasionally, his conscience pricked him: in 1852, for instance, he was "shocked" by the realization that he was spending $1,200 a year. But in the end he decided that his prolonged Grand Tour was well worth the money. "Here I am," he explained to brother George, "seeing the world in general & Europe in particular, learning languages, getting my health . . . making lots of first-class acquaintances . . . and all at the trifling expense of twelve hundred dollars a year!" Meanwhile, Andrew's management of John's money was so successful that John felt he could afford to donate a hundred dollars to the Home and Foreign Mission societies. Financially and socially these were De Forest's best days.[12]

When J. W. De Forest arrived in Europe, he was something of a provincial. He believed that Angelica Kauffman was a better painter than Titian or Raphael; after a year of visiting museums in England, France, Italy, and Germany, he still swore that Wilhelm Leutze's painting of Washington crossing the Delaware was "the grandest & noblest modern picture that I have ever seen." De Forest was a novice not only in the art gallery but also in the drawing room. When asked to participate in a pantomime with a group of Italians, he felt that his "northern stiffness" jarred harshly with the grace of the Latins. It was, ironically, in Calvinist Geneva that the Yankee first ventured onto a dance floor; and the spectacle of his awkward efforts, he said, would have made his brother split his sides with laughter.[13]

One of the most important lessons De Forest had to learn was that humility was a virtue consistently punished. When he acted with humble reserve, strangers treated him coolly, but when he approached them "in the brazen armor of self-assurance," they were friendly and admiring. "In this world," he discovered, "modesty is not appreciated & bashfulness is totally despised." He therefore practiced acting "as if I was really & indisputably the best man in every company where I come."[14] This winning brazenness was a quality that several of De Forest's fictional protagonists would have to acquire before they could reach their full stature as heroes. They would have to slough all meekness, act like men.

During these years, De Forest's religious ideas underwent a change—a broadening or a thinning, depending on one's point of view. Although De Forest continued to call himself "orthodox" in comparison to a nonbeliever, he now discarded much of the sectarianism and evangelicalism he had acquired as a child. By 1853 he was able to poke fun at his brother Henry's earnest proselytizing: "The Lord does not seem to be, by any means, so anxious to convert the Syrians as the missionaries are." By 1856, when he was back in America, he distressed a Congregational minister by asserting that God was unable to foresee events (an assertion the minister pronounced deistic, atheistic, and infidel). In *Witching Times,* De Forest's first novel, he drew a favorable portrait of Elder Higginson, whose sermons ignored "election, fore-ordination, special providences, damnation," and every other "savory doctrine." In "The Lauson Tragedy" (1870), he created a science professor named Henry Foster who seemed to present De Forest's own views:

> "Don't you believe in the God of Abraham, Isaac, and Jacob?" demanded Miss Mercy, striking home with telling directness.
> "I believe [said Foster] in a Deity who views his whole universe with equal love. I believe in a Deity greater than I always hear preached. . . ."
> "What are your opinions on the inspiration of the Scriptures?" she asked. . . .

"Miss Lauson, there are some subjects, indeed there are many subjects, on which I have no fixed opinions."[15]

De Forest's religion was more concerned with life on earth than with any afterlife. In his writings, God did not intervene in human affairs with "special providences," but He did affect people in less obtrusive ways. Those who believed in Him were honest, sober, meek, and kind, and when misfortune befell them, they cheered themselves by reading scripture and praying. Religion thus played two roles, both of a social rather than transcendental nature: it set standards of morality, and it comforted the suffering. De Forest seems to have believed in heaven (or at least some sort of pleasant regrouping after death) and to have doubted hell, but he did not devote much speculation to either. Anything otherworldly was beyond his purview.[16]

De Forest had moved a long way from the simple, certain Christianity of his mother. When, in 1868, he wrote an article depicting the typical girl of thirty years earlier, he probably used his mother as a model, and he portrayed her religious life with the smiling tolerance of a self-assured skeptic. The old-fashioned girl, he said, read little but devotional literature, attended church thrice on Sunday, taught Bible class, distributed tracts, and "held that it would be wicked to marry an 'unbeliever.'"[17] De Forest's placement of the word *unbeliever* within a cage of quotation marks suggests that he did not share the religious scrupulosity of the old-fashioned girl. As he moved from boyhood to manhood, he drifted into a passionless, comfortable, unphilosophical form of Christianity, the latitudinarianism of his father.

"Seeing the world" was one of De Forest's objectives when he went to Europe; "getting my health" was another. Puffing on the *argeeleh* in Syria had relieved his bronchial condition only temporarily, and "the fretting enmity of a monotonous invalidism" drove him to extreme measures. On the advice of the sculptor Horatio Greenough, whom he met in Florence, he entered Vincenz Priessnitz's famous water cure at Graefenberg in Silesia. Though skeptical at first, De Forest soon became a believer in *Kaltwasserkur.* His throat healed so fully, his voice grew so strong and deep, people could no longer tell that he had a bronchial ailment. "Hurrah for cold water!" he cried.[18]

Though designed for the weak in body, the treatment at Graefenberg did not appeal to the faint of heart. At least four times a day, the patients were plunged into cisterns of water, then "packed" in cold, wet sheets. Fed such simple food as milk and bread, they were forced to exercise rigorously: walking and running in the cool, damp, breezy alpine air. De Forest thrived on such a regimen, finding "a gradual increase of strength, a hitherto unknown power of enduring fatigue." To the habitual invalid, he said, there could be no sensation "more glorious, more superhuman, than the consciousness of abounding and sufficient strength." The relief was not merely physical but also psychological. As a chronically ill young man, De Forest might consider himself a weakling; but as a practitioner of *Kaltwasserkur*, he could think of himself as something of a hero. He prided himself on learning to discard his woolen garments and to wear only thin linen ones, even out of doors. He and other patients, he said, "caught no colds, and were savagely indifferent to our comforts." He believed that hardship brought out the best in him: courage, discipline, and stamina.[19]

On the other hand, he wanted more food and less rain; so after two months, "before my cure was half completed," he set out to find a new hydropathic physician. Moving to Divonne, France, on the Swiss frontier, he spent nearly eight months at the spa there and was "raised by the chill potency of pure water to as high a degree of health as is the ordinary award of mortals." In one respect, however, he was disappointed. At Divonne the treatment was much less Spartan than at Graefenberg: the patients wore less wet toweling and more dry clothing. "Fanaticized as I was by the savage enthusiasm of Graefenberg," said De Forest, "I secretly mourned over this effeminacy." Although he chose the water cure that offered greater comfort, he retained a sentimental longing for heroic austerity.[20]

Meanwhile, De Forest was writing. He had gone to Europe with literary ambitions, planning to research a history of the Italian republics and to write travel pieces for magazines, but once overseas, he struck out along new lines—verse. By August 1852 he had completed a volume of poems and submitted it to the American publisher Putnam and Griswold.[21]

Suspecting that his family would not approve this transition from history and journalism to the even less remunerative and more presumptuous enterprise of poetry, he explained it as a practical necessity. He had wanted to do historical research, he told Andrew, but had been balked by his deficiency in Latin. Discouraged about his prospects as a historian, he had decided to try writing "novels, nonsense & poetry" instead and had soon "flung off" a few verses. To brother George, De Forest offered a similarly apologetic explanation: possessing neither the documentary materials for history nor the journals from which to distill a travel book,[22] he had turned to poetry as a last resort. "I found out," he said, "almost by accident, that I had the faculty of rhyming, & I began to amuse myself with that . . . & often in the midst of my cogitations, this idea would come to tickle me: what if I should be a poet! I turned & examined this humorous supposition so often & so long, that, at last, it began to have the air of a reality."[23]

A humorous supposition indeed—De Forest's verses were rejected by Putnam and Griswold, and the author himself admitted that "the odor of Parnassus is not very strong in them." Nevertheless, he continued writing poems and by December 1853 was at work on a second volume. By this time, however, his rationale for versifying had changed: he still saw poetry as a necessity, but now for psychological reasons rather than practical ones. He had made a futile attempt, he told Andrew, to write prose—history, biography, romance, and philosophy—a failure due not to a dearth of materials but to a lack of inspiration or even interest. Although "I have no exalted hopes of success," he said, "I go on rhyming simply because I cannot bear to do anything else." By late 1853, De Forest's sense of a calling had strengthened sufficiently so that he no longer explained his work as accidental.[24]

In light of his later career, it is worth noting that J. W. De Forest attempted poetry before fiction, that he became a novelist only after failing as a poet, that he viewed the writing of prose as a last resort. De Forest had been reared in a family in which poetry was respectable but fiction was not. John Hancock De Forest's library included Shakespeare, Milton, Cowper, and Pope, but the only novel he is known to have possessed was *Don Quixote*. He seems to have detested the fiction of his own day. When his son George went away to school in 1825, John Hancock De Forest urged him to occupy his evenings with study, then added: "At any rate you must not read novels." Poetry was the language of the ancients, the universally recognized greats; the novel was novel, prose was prosaic. In later years, J. W. De Forest would describe "a Puritan mother and a Roman father" who "deigned to own few books which had not been read and approved by their ancestors" and who allowed their child to read only such worthies as Shakespeare, Milton, Cowper, and Pope. Raised with the idea that poetry was immortal, De Forest would not stoop readily to the writing of prose.[25]

Nevertheless, he exaggerated somewhat when he said he could not bear desisting from rhyme. There was one thing, at least, that could lead him back to prose—money. While asserting that "a man cannot write without being interested in his subject," he added an important qualifier: "unless, indeed, he is driven to it day after day by want of bread." If ever he should find himself in that condition, De Forest said, "then I will resume prose." In the coming years, the writer would often be in want of bread and, for its sake, would abandon not only poetry but also much else in which he was genuinely "interested."[26]

In 1854 or 1855, De Forest returned to America, his Grand Tour finally ended. Settling in a hotel in New Haven, he made use of his travels by writing *Oriental Acquaintance,* a report of his experiences in the Levant. He meanwhile made a new and most important acquaintance in New Haven—Harriet Silliman Shepard.[27]

Miss Shepard was one of those women who pass their lives in the shadow of a prominent man. In her case the man was her father, Dr. Charles Upham Shepard. (Her mother, also named Harriet, died in October 1854.) A first cousin of Ralph Waldo

Emerson; a former student of natural history at Brown, Amherst, and Harvard; a former colleague of Benjamin Silliman the elder at Yale; and a founder of the phosphate industry in South Carolina—Dr. Shepard had an international reputation as a mineralogist. In 1855 Dr. Shepard held joint appointments as professor of chemistry at Amherst College in Massachusetts and at Charleston Medical College in South Carolina. Besides migrating annually between Amherst and Charleston, the peripatetic scientist maintained a cottage in New Haven and traveled occasionally to Europe. A popular lecturer on the subject of manners and a freethinker, he was the sort of urbane iconoclast who would appeal to J. W. De Forest. He also had a pretty daughter.[28]

Harriet Shepard was an ornament of society. Born November 23, 1833, she was seven years younger than De Forest. She was both comely and well-bred, and she knew how to have a good time. She enjoyed dances, dinners, fine clothing, novels, travel, visiting, and all sorts of public entertainments; one afternoon in 1856, her aunt found her "lying on the sofa fagged out by partys." She had a reputation as a linguist, and she could read *The Count of Monte Cristo* in French. This is not to say, however, that she was a heavy thinker. Her letters reflect no extraordinary alacrity or profundity of mind, and her commonplace book shows that her taste in poetry ran toward the sentimental. De Forest probably used Miss Shepard as the model when he described the heroine of *Miss Ravenel's Conversion*: "She was not a learned woman, nor an unpleasantly strong-minded one, but an average young lady of good breeding—just such as most men fall in love with [—] who wanted social success, and depended for it upon pretty looks and pleasant ways."[29]

Pretty looks and pleasant ways were enough for De Forest. By May of 1855, he was sufficiently smitten to be sending Miss Shepard his poems, which she then inserted amidst the other maudlin verses in her commonplace book. De Forest's affection for her may not have been entirely blind—one of the poems he sent her was titled "To a Coquette"—nevertheless, he pursued the courtship with diligence. In November 1855 Dr. Shepard headed south to perform his duties at Charleston Medical College, and his daughter, as always, went with him. This time, however, they had a fellow traveler.[30]

De Forest was not thinking only of Miss Shepard, however. As long as he was in the Deep South, a place as exotic to a New Englander as Syria or France, he observed it with the eye of a reporter. He asked his family to save his letters from South Carolina, as they had saved those from Syria, so that he might use them later as sources for a book. Obviously De Forest was planning ahead—and planning a career as a writer.[31]

De Forest particularly scrutinized the South's peculiar institution. Having grown up during the national debate over slavery, he had previously taken notice of free blacks in New England as well as on the other side of the Atlantic. In Turkey, for instance, he had seen a handsomely dressed, dignified, intelligent black who personified self-respect. "I saw at once," said the visitor, "that he had been treated like a man all his life, and that not the least suspicion had ever entered his brain that he was not a man. He gave me new ideas of the possibilities of the African race." At about the same time that these words were getting into print, however, De Forest was acquiring or strengthening a much less flattering impression of blacks. Upon arriving in Charleston, he found the bondsmen stupider than he had imagined, with small heads and "generally a childish if not a slightly animal air." Though better behaved than the free blacks of the North, the slaves were equally ragged in dress; moreover, he said, they were contented in their condition of servitude. More sniggering was done by the "darkies" of Charleston, he maintained, than by all the whites of Connecticut, and he could not imagine that such "inexpressible gaiety" could be combined with unhappiness.[32]

In South Carolina, De Forest was struck for the first time by what he called "the favorable side of slavery," having heard only about the other side while in the North. Finding blacks less intelligent and more contented than he had expected, he believed that "they are not worth all the hulabaloo that is made about them." He agreed with the abolitionists that the institution of slavery kept the bondsmen "ignorant & animal," but he asseverated with mathematical precision that their great-great-grand-fathers in Africa had been four times as ignorant and twice as animal. In short, the blacks—despite being enslaved—were making about as much progress as could be expected.[33]

Further experience in the South provided De Forest with a somewhat different impression of the slaves' condition. A month and a half after reporting their "inexpressible gaiety," De Forest wrote that the "niggers" were "saucy & turbulent, and getting more so every year." Encouraged by blacks who had lived near the free states, the slaves were growing increasingly rebellious. A century hence, the writer feared, "the nameless people may have a name written in blood and fire." Although De Forest came to realize the slaves' discontent, he never wished them sudden and total liberation; instead, he hoped that slavery would be eradicated very slowly, transformed into a form of serfdom that would eventually give way to freedom. This process would take 150 years, six generations, "a period not at all too lengthy when we consider Quashee's present laziness and stupidity." De Forest thus showed his distaste for slavery by proposing its abolition, but he expressed his disdain for slaves by pushing that abolition into a comfortably distant future.[34]

De Forest's appreciation of "the favorable side of slavery" alarmed his family in New England, and they warned him against "the seductions of slavery." The traveler responded with a "confession of orthodoxy": "I am stiff as far as the politics of the matter are concerned, as well as on the remote question of justice or injustice. I believe in Free Soil, Kansas squatters, Sharp's rifles, & Mr. Seward." Moreover, he castigated apostate Yankees who came South and bought slaves even though they had previously deplored the institution. While staying clear of radical abolitionism, De Forest also refrained from becoming an apologist for slavery.[35]

For De Forest, 1856 was a turning point or, perhaps, the point of no return. In the spring, he left Charleston for New Haven, and on June 5 he married Harriet Shepard. During that same year, *Oriental Acquaintance* was published as a book, and *Putnam's Monthly Magazine* began serializing *Witching Times*. In this, the year of the Pottawatomie Massacre and the caning of Charles Sumner, J. W. De Forest committed himself to such quiet pursuits as raising a family and writing novels.[36]

De Forest's marriage was not without its pleasures. Harriet was a fun-loving woman, and she and John shared such amusements as public lectures, social calls, and buggy rides. One day in 1861, John, Harriet, her brother and sister, and a dog named Jack were enjoying themselves so much that Harriet's uncle, a dour Congregational minister, disgustedly described them as "all cutting up as only demented people real maniacs would!"[37]

Despite these occasional good times, however, it seems that the De Forests' marriage was not a happy one. They left no diaries or letters explicitly discussing their life together, but circumstantial evidence suggests that it was frequently troubled and decidedly sporadic. To begin with, there was the fact that Harriet seemed to prefer the company of her father to that of her husband. Two winters after her wedding, she was still accompanying Dr. Shepard on his annual trek to Charleston, even though John remained in New Haven; and she was hoping that in the coming year John would undertake a visit to California by himself. Her uncle, Rev. George C. Shepard, sarcastically noted in his diary that Harriet was "a very contented & happy *widow*" who was "not given to melancholly [sic] at being separated from her *dear* husband." Despite such criticism, however, the couple continued going their separate ways. The following winter, John was ice skating near New Haven while his wife was reading novels in Charleston. In 1860 and again in 1871 or 1872, Harriet accompanied her father on a trip to Europe, but John stayed home. When Harriet Shepard De Forest died, she was with her father in Charleston. Her husband was elsewhere.[38]

Harriet and John seem to have argued over the importance of their respective families. The Shepards and the De Forests were both old, distinguished New England clans, but the Shepards were a little older and perhaps a little more distinguished. Again the evidence is merely circumstantial, but it suggests that Harriet made invidious comparisons and that John resented them. In a novel published in 1878, De Forest had a character, a woman, say: "I believe it is a common weakness of women to be conceited about their own family, and to hold that their husbands and their husbands' relatives are nobodies." In the same novel, a woman advised her daughter never to "drive your husband deaf and mad" by boasting of her family. Charles Shepard was a renowned scientist, J. W. De Forest an obscure novelist. It is likely that Harriet Shepard De Forest noticed the difference, and it is possible that this was one reason she often went with her father and left her husband behind.[39]

Mrs. De Forest also may have spent her winters in the South to avoid the frosty weather of New England—her health, like her husband's, was frequently poor—and this chronic illness probably caused further discontent in the marriage. In 1856 she was fainting, vomiting, nervous, and cold; in 1861 she was bedridden with congestion of the lungs, "catarrhal Fever," and what was professionally diagnosed as "nervousness"; in 1863 her uncle reported that she was inclined to "play sick a good deal." The Rev. Mr. Shepard may have been unduly skeptical: the fact that Mrs. De Forest died suddenly in 1878 at the age of forty-four suggests that her frail health was not entirely "play." Nevertheless, whether her illnesses were physiological, psychogenic, or merely pretended, they surely were inconvenient. One morning when she did not come to the table to eat, her uncle recorded that "her husband had to get & carry to her her breakfast in bed. I pity him & dislike her conduct." It is altogether possible that De Forest shared those sentiments.[40]

Money was another problem—a big one. Mrs. De Forest, it seems, was accustomed to expensive forms of leisure. The sight of her on a shopping expedition in 1857 was enough to drive her clergyman-uncle to righteous fury:

> She was dressed up like a simpleton ready to enter a Ball Room—She had on an enormous Pine *Apple* dress! She is a very clever good natured wom[an] over all till she comes to *dress*—That has stolen her heart—If she loved her God at all as she loves a Bonnet or her husband & child as she does dress she would be angelic. But as it is, if she gets through the world in this style and never feels crushing want I am no prophet.

Eight years later, Rev. Shepard noted that the one thing that could cure Mrs. De Forest's sickness and get her out of bed was the opportunity to go shopping: "Better than a physician, yet expensive."[41]

De Forest himself did not leave behind any written criticism of his wife's spending, unless one counts the diatribes against female extravagance that pepper his published works. His most thorough discussion of the theme appeared in the article "Two Girls," in which he compared the "Puritan maiden" of thirty years earlier (who had much in common with De Forest's mother) with the "modern girl" of the present (who bore a resemblance to De Forest's wife). The former, he said, wore simple, home-made clothes; the latter spent large sums on ornate and ugly attire. The former cost her husband little; the latter crushed him under debts. As one solution to the problem of the spendthrift modern girl, De Forest proposed that she get a job. If she were employed, she would add to the family income; if she were drawing wages, she would learn the value of money and the need for economy; if she were working hard, she might become healthier; and if she were kept busy, she would have less opportunity to spend—such was De Forest's plan for the reformation of the household economy.[42] In his own household, however, the reform did not occur. There is no evidence that Harriet De Forest ever worked a day, earned a penny, or ceased to purchase dresses that resembled pineapples.

In addition to the obsessive denunciation of free-spending females, De Forest's writings provide further circumstantial evidence of marital discord. Four years after his wedding, for example, he wrote "Henry Gilbert," a tale in which a "cheerful, gentle, irrepressible girl" gets married, then grows full of "fretfulness and complainings . . . suspicions . . . gloom or spitefulness." Even more suggestive is the unpublished manuscript version of a poem, which includes these verses:

> We play like children at a game;
> We mimic out the game of life;
> We prattle words like *love* & *wife*
> Whose fire should set the heart aflame.

We mean not anything we say;
    There is no purpose in this choice,
    Far less than in the tinkling voice
Of birds who chatter in the spray.

Words like *love* and *wife* might very well seem meaningless to a man whose spouse frequently lived far away. In the novel *The Bloody Chasm,* De Forest depicted a husband and wife who, at the wife's insistence, live apart. Of this strange arrangement, the wife's aunt says, "A lady should do almost anything, rather than live separated. I am of the old-fashioned sort. I believe that marriage should mean something." It is hard to believe that De Forest was not equally old-fashioned.[43]

If De Forest ever told his wife what he hated most about her, he probably said that she was more self-centered, self-indulgent, and willful than any woman had a right to be. De Forest believed that a true woman lived for others, not for herself. A woman had, he said, "the patience of the lower animals and of inanimate nature, ennobled by a heavenly joy of self-sacrifice, a divine pleasure in suffering for those whom she loves." Harriet De Forest had many pleasures, but suffering was not one of them. She bought whatever dress or bonnet struck her fancy, she would not tie herself down to a job, she traveled with her father to South Carolina and Europe, and she left her husband to take care of himself. De Forest probably thought of his fun-loving wife when he wrote that it is a "selfish woman" who lives " 'to enjoy herself' and to 'have a good time.' "[44]

Divorce was sometimes on De Forest's mind, but for a gentleman it was unthinkable. In *The Bloody Chasm,* the husband is a gentleman and "doesn't choose to dishonor himself, and publish his dishonor to the world"; while the wife "shan't ask for a divorce. No South Carolina lady ever did." As the wife's aunt says, "It is a thing that niggers and Yankees do."[45] De Forest was a Yankee, but an old-fashioned one. He was not about to become a modern instance.

The coolness between John and Harriet De Forest may relate in some fashion to the fact that they had only one child. On

February 23, 1857, Harriet gave birth to a boy who, after being threatened with the names Victor Hugo and Cotton Mather, was eventually christened Louis Shepard De Forest. Although the baby may have been somewhat premature (arriving eight and a half months after the wedding), the birth seems to have been a normal one. The letters and diaries by Mrs. De Forest's relatives do not mention her having any difficulty giving birth, and the "hopeful child" himself was soon being described as "fat and good tempered."[46] There is thus no known reason why the De Forests could not have had more children. The fact is, however, that they did not, perhaps because of the wife's chronic sickness, perhaps because of a lack of ardor on someone's part.

Then again, perhaps the De Forests did not want another child. Harriet, a fashionable woman who insisted on hiring a wet nurse for baby Louis, may not have wished to be tied down by offspring. John, who always had writing to do, seems to have viewed children as an irritating distraction. In July 1857 George Shepard reported that four-month-old Louis was making the house "lively"; in that same month, De Forest published a story called "The Baby Exterminator" that, with considerable enthusiasm, described a machine for smothering noisy, inquisitive infants. Apparently, De Forest had little affection for children. His novels frequently portray them as brats badly in need of a whipping; they figure among the vilest villains of *Witching Times*. Although in later years De Forest would prove sufficiently paternal to teach his boy to play cards (much to the chagrin of Rev. Shepard), father and son never became close. Decades later Louis would describe his father as "a silent, distant man."[47]

De Forest seems to have seen himself in much the same way. In the novel *Seacliff*, for example, the hero—who in many ways bears a likeness to the author—fears that he is "an unloving man, incapable of earnest affection for women." In his last published novel, De Forest says that a mature man "longs to love even more than he longs to be loved"; and in the tale "The Hungry Heart" (1870), a man's lack of sentiment drives his wife to adultery, then suicide. Harriet De Forest never went quite that far, but she did go to Charleston.[48]

De Forest's detachment from his wife and child may have had at least one good effect: it gave him plenty of time to write. In 1856 he published *Oriental Acquaintance* and *Witching Times,* and for the next five years he worked hard to perfect his craft. As Mrs. De Forest's uncle reported approvingly, "He is very industrious, never gossiping or sitting among the idle and dissipated."[49]

Witching Times was De Forest's first book-length fiction, but in many respects it was a continuation of his historical studies. Superficially it was the story of two young lovers overcoming sudden obstacles to true happiness, but fundamentally, as its title indicates, it was a historical analysis of the Salem witchcraft episode of 1692. De Forest had read Cotton Mather, Robert Calef, and other historians, and now he offered his own interpretation of the crisis. He portrayed it as the product of a conjunction of human vices: the superstition of the common folk, the mischievousness of children, and the lust, ambition, and vindictiveness of individual accusers. Just as De Forest had examined the Indians of Connecticut, described their decline, and explained its causes, he now turned his scientific attention to the Puritans of Massachusetts and their tragic folly. Throughout his career he would have less success in telling the story of a few individuals than in describing the environment in which the story occurred. It was no accident that he began his career by working in a genre as loosely plotted as history.

De Forest's preference for setting rather than plot was apparent again in his next two books. *European Acquaintance* (1858), his second travel book, was another collection of literary sketches taken during his Grand Tour. *Seacliff* (1859), his second novel, was an implausible mystery story grafted onto the inevitable tale of young people in love; but it was redeemed by De Forest's gift for shrewd observation. Turning away from both history and travel, he located the novel in contemporary America and studied the scene with the assiduity that he had previously devoted to the Massachusetts Bay Colony and the Orient. He noted, for example, one thoroughly modern fellow who "reposed as an anaconda might, his small head laying against the back of a rocking-chair, while his lank body rested on the outer edge of the seat, and his extremities stretched far away into the middle of the room. The American is the only man who knows what to do with the small of his back. He sits on it. No other nation has made this discovery." In this same ironic way De Forest pointed out the "transitory and migratory" character of umbrellas, the marvelous fact being that "innumerable individuals have lost one, but nobody ever seems to have found one."[50]

From the standpoint of biography, *Seacliff* is most interesting for its portrayal of the artist as an aging young man. The novel's protagonist is a writer, Louis Fitz Hugh, who reflects the professional aspirations, doubts, and frustrations of his creator. Like De Forest, Fitz Hugh has spent many years abroad, has written a book about his travels, but has not made much of a mark in the world. He knows that "to be distinguished young is a godlike lot which falls to few" and that he was not one of those few. Nevertheless, he has not surrendered his dreams. More than anything else, he wishes that he could "be full young once more, and yet possess all the power and energy of maturity. . . . If that dream could be granted me, then would I waste no time in pleasure, none in idleness, none, as now, in despair, but gathering all my intellectual and emotional nature into one effort, I would produce a work in literature that should make me famous at once." These large ambitions, however, are not placed on public view. When asked what sort of work he intends to undertake now that he has returned to America, Fitz Hugh is embarrassed.

> "But what are you going to do in America, Mr. Fitz Hugh?" she resumed. "What great labors are you going to perform, to make amends for your European idleness?"
>
> Now I really intended to become an author, having already got a book of travels on the launching-ways of a New York publisher, and having projected at least half a dozen other works in history, biography, and romance, with which I meant to storm the world's attention. But I naturally objected to making an ostentation of these facts—and so I replied simply that I was engaged in a course of private study.

Like De Forest, who in 1848 had vehemently denied being "carried away by a fancy for being something out of the ordinary," Fitz Hugh modestly conceals immodest aspirations.[51]

In 1859, when *Seacliff* was published, De Forest had reasons for concealment. He had been writing for more than a decade, but he still had relatives who wanted him to pursue a more practical career. Although Dr. Charles Shepard encouraged his son-in-law by calling him "the best writer of modern times," Rev. George Shepard better represented the consensus of the De Forest family and in-laws. In 1857 the minister predicted that De Forest would never make "the first red cent" through "his silly efforts at book writing." Sounding like De Forest's brother Andrew in 1848, Shepard also predicted that, after another unprofitable year or two, "he will then understand himself & his capabilities better than he does now." Half a year later, the preacher said that De Forest's *European Acquaintance* was "*a waste of time*" and contained "*vulgarities* enough, to destroy his reputation among refined and intellectual people." Doubting that the book would yield even five dollars in royalties, Shepard hoped that De Forest might find some more remunerative employment—sorting rags, for instance. Although Rev. Shepard's critique may have been uncommonly pungent, it seems to have represented the attitude of most of the Shepards and De Forests. According to the novelist's grandson, "the family did not take my grandfather's work very seriously because he never made a living out of writing." Judged by dollar signs, De Forest's work was a failure. How, then, could he tell his family that writing was his calling?[52]

How, indeed, could he tell himself? By 1859 De Forest had reached another crisis. He, like Louis Fitz Hugh, still wanted "to storm the world's attention" as an author; but he, too, wasted much time in "despair." He was thirty-three years old, had a wife and a child, and still was making almost no money from his writings. Living partly off income from his inheritance and partly off largesse from his father-in-law, De Forest must have seen himself as a parasite, particularly when he compared himself to his brothers George, the bank president, and Andrew, the lumber company owner. (Henry, the medical missionary, had died in 1858.) Then, too, De Forest must have been uncomfortably aware of the precariousness of his finances. So dependent was he on Dr. Shepard that, according to Rev. Shepard, the doctor's illness for even one year would plunge De Forest, his wife, and his child into "a helpless degree of want and misery."[53] By the time *Seacliff* was published, the novelist was thinking about some other way to make a living.

"Mr De Forest has caved in on *Book making*," announced George Shepard in November 1859. After years of writing that had yielded neither cash nor credit, De Forest had given up and had begun to look for a regular job. "He hung his hat too high at first," the minister gleefully reported. "It must be blowed or knocked down, & he must try again." De Forest was about to try on a new hat, one appropriate for the educated poor. He had agreed to edit a New Haven newspaper for a week and, if that worked out, to invest in the paper.[54] There is no record of how De Forest fared as an editor, but it does seem that he had "caved in" on the writing of fiction. In 1860 he published only two short stories, in 1861, none at all, and there is no evidence that he was working on another novel. By 1861 it seemed that De Forest might become a journalist, a small capitalist, a member of the productive classes. Earlier he had said that "want of bread" could drive a man from poetry to prose; now he was being driven from novels to newspapers. It seemed he might become just another novelist manqué.

But then the war came.

Chapter 3

My forte is tittle-tattle concerning living men.

J. W. De Forest, *European Acquaintance,* 1858

J. W. De Forest's first five books were a disparate lot: a history, two travel books, two novels. Despite their differences in genre, however, they had certain common themes, certain topics they brought up again and again. In a sense, all five books dealt with the same general topic: modern civilization. When De Forest described Indians or Puritans, he did so in order to compare them to people of the present. When he described Oriental or European acquaintances, he considered them as representatives of ancient ways of life and compared them to the modern people of the United States. (One's own country always exists in the present, but foreign countries often exist in the past, occasionally in the future.) When De Forest made these comparisons—between the past and the present, the Old World and the New—he fell with easy regularity into the condition known as nostalgia.

Nostalgia is a pleasing form of pain. One inflicts it on oneself to interrupt the comfortable monotony of daily life. It adds poignancy to an existence that otherwise might be nothing but happy. It adds dimension. One deliberately seeks it out, sets one's mind to imagining other times, other people, indulges in a few rich moments of desire, then, sadly, remembers that one belongs in the present day. There is something fraudulent, however, about that sadness. It is regulated, exactly controlled; it never erupts into anguish, bitterness, rage, or despair. One submits to such a sadness only long enough to give one's life a meretricious tang of tragedy, then, suddenly, one turns the sentiment off. That is the difference between nostalgia and grief.

De Forest's first books were exercises in nostalgia. He lived in the nineteenth century, and he found much to admire in modern times. He believed the people were productive, self-reliant, honest, enlightened, humane, about as good as people had ever been. Even goodness, however, grows wearisome eventually. Just for relief, De Forest directed his thoughts back to witching times in Massachusetts, Indian times in Connecticut, and feudal times in Europe and the Levant. There he found something new—or, rather, exotically old—to admire: bravery, chivalry, imagination. He wished that modern men possessed equal heroism. He lamented their degeneracy. Yet, he did not really wish to live in the past. Like any other victim of nostalgia, he finally repudiated his illusions and escaped from the pain of imagination. When all was said and done, he was glad to get back into the commonplace fact of the present.

All things considered, J. W. De Forest was pleased with the way the universe was turning out. The human race was getting better all the time. For example, people of the nineteenth century were showing admirable energy, restless industry, productivity. The son and brother of successful entrepreneurs, De Forest believed that his age was building a new and ever-richer civilization. He praised the music of enterprise: the sound of "busy multitudes, . . . the strokes of the printing press, the puff of the steamboat, and the thundering rush of the locomotive," not only the familiar pastoral lowing of cattle but also the new industrial "hum and clatter of machinery." To him, the world seemed to be moving forward economically, commercially, and technologically; in a word, improving.[1]

Such progress, he believed, depended not so much on the natural resources of a country as on the character of the people themselves. With no little satisfaction, he viewed his countrymen as a peculiarly sturdy and hard-working lot. Other peoples, however, seemed moribund. So it was with the ancient Indians of Connecticut who, according to De Forest, left the forests unbroken except by "the long-drawn howl of the wolf and the piercing yell of the panther." Nor were Native Americans the only ones who left the land a wilderness. *Oriental Acquaintance* begins with a description of a landing in Turkey, which vividly makes the point:

> The trim Boston bark which had brought me safely, though tediously tempest-beaten, from the low green shores of Massachusetts, at last lay at anchor in the Bay of Smyrna. Before my western eyes were spread out, in oriental strangeness, the shabby wharves, the fragile minarets, and the rough red-tiled roofs of the Queen of Ionia. . . . The boat was let down from the side, and, in my solitary dignity as only passenger, I descended the ladder with the captain, and was rowed ashore. The falling timbers of a ruinous wooden quay, symbolical, in their rottenness, of the people and government of the country, gave me footing on the shore of Turkey.

The contrast between the "trim Boston bark"—emblem of vigor, adventure, speed—and the "shabby wharves" of Smyrna summarizes the difference between the New World and the Old. Throughout the book, De Forest draws similar comparisons, and he concludes with a scene intended to show the utter stupor and paralysis of the Orient. In Syria a group of Americans finds a sordid little village squatting amidst the crumbling walls of what centuries earlier had been a great city built by the Byzantines. Noticing all the heavy building stones scattered about, one American asks,

> "Why do you not take these fine stones and build yourself a better village?"
> "O, Howaja," replied the feeble barbarians, "these stones are too large; we cannot lift them."
> And there we left them, beneath the heavy walls, whose strength, even in ruin, mocked at their savage impotence.

Savage impotence, feeble barbarism—what a contrast to the creative energy of modern civilization.[2]

Part of the savages' problem was their religion. Although De Forest never attempted to describe the exact process by which a religion generated either indolence or initiative in its adherents, he had no doubt that it did. On the Turkish-controlled island of Rhodes, he observed "sterility & desolation" and concluded that "such is the influence of the crescent [of Islam] everywhere." Catholicism, too, was counterproductive. In France, De Forest contrasted Protestant villages with Catholic ones, finding the former "tidy, solidly built, nicely whitewashed . . . and inhabited by broad, burly, vigorous men," while a Catholic town like Divonne, "blessed with the true Church, holy water, the Bishop of Freiburg, and all these orthodox advantages, was as mean, dirty a little village as you shall see marring the beauty of a summer's day." In Italy, the fountainhead of Catholicism, De Forest found the people "good-for-nothing, . . . always idle and useless." Catholicism, like Mohammedanism, fostered moral (and, hence, economic) decay. Viewing all this, De Forest must have been glad to be a Protestant from the land of steady habits.[3]

In addition to breeding indolence, Catholicism also demoralized people by undermining their self-respect. In his writings, De Forest consistently praised the individualist who not only provided for himself in a material way but also thought well enough of himself to act independently, without undue regard for the opinions and actions of others. In *Witching Times,* the rational Henry More opposes almost single-handedly the superstitious "masses," the "gang" of witch hunters; he always does what he knows is right, while the "doughfaces" drift with public opinion. In a later, whimsical article about cats, De Forest praised them for being "useful but not slavish"; they earned their keep by catching rats, but they could not be ordered about like dogs. De Forest, who kept cats, called the cat an ally rather than a servant, but called the dog a "humble boot-licker and toady." When he described a shabby Jewish guide in *Oriental Acquaintance,* he showed his contempt for doglike submissiveness: "If you only looked at him, he would, as it were, sneak to your feet, and, with his whole air and soul, grovel in the dust. I felt as if I wanted to kick him, but did not do so, [for] fear of dirtying my boots." This Jew on the island of Rhodes had much in common with Catholics throughout the world. Papism, De Forest believed, stifled self-reliance by teaching blind obedience to ecclesiastical authority. He was disgusted by the way Romans kissed the feet of the pontiff, and De Forest suggested that they instead "set teeth into the fat legs" of their spiritual overseers. Trusting the individual's private search for truth, and skeptical of rituals led by priests, he lamented that no bookstore in Florence carried an inexpensive edition of "that anti-papal publication," the Bible. In later years, he would write a series of articles depicting the sinister history of "Giant Pope."[4]

One evil consequence of Catholics' supposed willingness to toady to authority was the impossibility of republican government. To dispense with a monarch, the people of a nation had to have self-respect: to trust their own judgment, to chart their own course, to bear responsibility. But Catholicism, De Forest believed, destroyed individualism and thereby turned men into a helpless herd who needed to be led. Living in France when Louis Napoleon subverted the French Republic, De Forest told his brother that the great mass of French peasants and villagers "neither know nor care anything about politics, & blindly follow the direction of this or that priest, this or that leader." The old religion had corrupted its followers, he said, and corrupt men could not have good government. Only if Romanism were overthrown could republicanism prevail. Such a purge, said the Connecticut Yankee, was the "only hope."[5]

Besides being lazy, obsequious, and unrepublican, Catholics were distinctly unkind. In 1851 De Forest observed "the heartlessness of much, if not all, of catholic society," and in his subsequent fictions—most notably in the characterization of Madame Larue in *Miss Ravenel's Conversion*—he frequently portrayed Catholics as smiling monsters, amiable in manner but entirely selfish. De Forest's first published article and his last published book of prose both detailed the Catholic persecution of Protestants during the Counter Reformation—"the scaffold and the stake." The "heartlessness" of Catholics was not something he could forget.[6]

Of course, not every ruthless human being took communion in the Church of Rome. The Indians of Connecticut, as De Forest described them, were vengeful, bloodthirsty, and sadistic, and the Puritans who fought them were much the same. After reporting on how a band of Pequots was "massacred in cold blood," De Forest lamented the "fanaticism and sternness" of the Puritans and observed, "They were not behind their age in gentleness indeed, but it is to be feared that they were very little in advance of it." It was these same fanatical and stern Puritans who strung up people accused of witchery—another example of this strange civilization. De Forest was appalled by the ferocity of all barbarians, whether Indian, Puritan, or Catholic.[7]

Barbarism manifested itself not only in cruelty but also in irrationality. In his early writings, De Forest took primitive peoples to task for their insusceptibility to reason, particularly in matters of religion. Much of *Oriental Acquaintance* was given over to exposing and lampooning the supposed mysteries of the Holy Land—magical rituals, sacred shrines, and the like. In *History of the Indians,* De Forest mocked the savages who worked themselves into religious frenzy, foaming at the mouth and writhing in the dust. He then extended the mockery to all those willing to "dethrone reason": the "howling dervishes" of Turkey, the pagans of the South Sea islands, and the "religious enthusiasts" who sometimes appeared in the Christian world. De Forest's short story "My Neighbor, the Prophet" (1860) ridiculed those who threw themselves "with childish faith into the arms of the supernatural." The story's narrator, a professor of geology, expressed what seems to be the author's own view: "I can't stand mysteries." In *European Acquaintance,* De Forest said it himself: "In a general way, I entertain very disrespectful opinions of modern miracles." As a rational man of the nineteenth century, he could look with contempt on earlier ages and on backward people who remained innocent of science.[8]

Exotic cultures gave De Forest one more issue for comparison with modern America, the matter of honesty. In Syria, De Forest found that the people seemed "good-natured" enough but that their behavior was spoiled by "a plentiful peppering of lies." In Catholic Europe, he found that people were wonderfully gracious but that graciousness often masked the most disgraceful deeds and intentions. In contrast, Americans (and their English cousins) might exhibit an unpleasant "gravity & coldness" of demeanor, but they had real love in their hearts, genuine good will. There was, De Forest believed, nothing fraudulent about a Yankee.[9]

In short, De Forest found plenty of reason to be pleased with the culture from which he came, at least when he compared it to other cultures. Americans were energetic, independent, good-hearted, rational, and direct; other people were otherwise. His country and his age were about the best that had ever existed; or so he believed.

It was at just this point that nostalgia began creeping in. The modern man, as De Forest envisioned him, was busy, honest, reasonable, kind—in short, something of a bore. He possessed virtue, no doubt, but it was virtue in the modern, maidenly, law-abiding sense, not the simple strength of the ancients. De Forest ridiculed men of old for being "fanatics," but at times he found that same fanaticism appealing. He found beauty in the Old World's obsessive refinement of manners, and he found nobility in the recklessness of savages. J. W. De Forest was a moderate man, but sometimes he dreamt of extremes.

Europe was the homeland of exaggerated etiquette. As De Forest compared that continent to America, he could not help noticing and admiring the way in which Europeans made a fine art of mere deportment. In France, he talked with an old army captain and quoted him at length:

> "Manner is a great art, *Monsieur*; almost a nature, in fact; a man must acquire it so early that you may say it was born with him. Let him grow up without it, he never seizes it, no matter what society he keeps, and you can detect him for a native boor the moment he enters a drawing-room. Yes, *Monsieur,* a man must be born to society, or he can not be worthy of it; he must have it in his blood, as it were."

De Forest enjoyed seeing exquisite manners and relished the people who had cultivated them to the highest degree, the European aristocrats. They were, he said, "the best behaved class of humanity that I have ever had the pleasure of observing." De Forest was aware, however, that fine etiquette, like aristocracy, was a thing of the past. The French captain was an old man who mourned the decline of the social graces in the modern world, and De Forest studied him attentively because "the captain was so evidently a relic of old times and old manners in France." De Forest's fascination with perfect manners reflected a longing for the lost, the past, the impossible.[10]

Like other forms of nostalgia, however, this one was easily

relieved. All De Forest had to do was to shift his attention from exquisite manners to other characteristics that necessarily accompanied those manners but that were not so attractive—idleness, for instance. To master the social graces, Europeans had to give them the attention Americans gave to productive labor; it was the aristocracy, the leisure class, that perfected etiquette. De Forest, however, had little respect for drones, no matter how beautifully behaved. He said that dandies who followed the fashionable life were "worthless to the world." Moreover, fine manners were associated in his mind with dishonesty. Savoir-faire and winsome geniality often served to disguise the most pernicious thoughts. Fine manners were thus coupled with uselessness and deceit. One had to choose between manners and morals.[11]

De Forest had no trouble making that choice, and in *Seacliff* he stated the matter clearly, albeit not artfully. Frank Somerville, a handsome, refined man of wealth and lineage, states the aristocratic position: "A gentleman of manners, . . . no matter how vicious, is a civilizer. He teaches people to be clean, to be tasteful, to speak good grammar, to avoid indecorums and so forth." But since Somerville later turns out to be a blackmailer, the reader must look elsewhere for a definitive pronouncement on the subject of manners. Louis Fitz Hugh, as usual, provides it. Though he acknowledges that Somerville's proposition is "to some extent correct," Fitz Hugh modifies it in an important way: "Great is urbanity, great is decorum, and almost worthy of being classed among the moralities." The crucial word is *almost*. Although manners are important, they are less so than morals. Though sentiment attracts an American to Europe, judgment drives him back home. Thus is nostalgia overcome.[12]

Fine manners, however, were not all that modern men had lost. More importantly, more regrettably, they had lost the capacity for heroism. During the decades of De Forest's youth and early middle age, it became commonplace for writers to lament that they lived in a prosaic epoch. From the 1820s to the 1850s, Americans compared themselves to the earlier, Revolutionary generation and suffered (quite literally) by the comparison. Realizing that they had not duplicated the bravery, the integrity, and the world-transforming success of the Founding Fathers, they perceived themselves as weaker people engaged in more trivial pursuits. The problem was not merely that the age could not match the heroism of the Revolutionary age; the problem was that it could not match the heroism of *any* previous age. Men of De Forest's time were picayune not only in comparison to the Founding Fathers but also in comparison to the Puritans, the Crusaders, the Romans—even, in some ways, to the American Indians. Modernity itself was the problem. In 1855 *Putnam's Monthly* published an article bewailing the present day's loss of "the heroic virtues, the chivalric sentiments." Later that same year, the magazine began publishing a serialized novel that also lamented the demise of those "heroic virtues," a novel entitled *Witching Times.*[13]

Perhaps it was inevitable that a man who reminded his sister-in-law of Richard Baxter would himself be fascinated by Puritans. In any case, the young De Forest wrote about them repeatedly, not only in *Witching Times* but also in *History of the Indians of Connecticut* and in the short story "The Isle of the Puritans" (1857). In all these tales, he portrayed the founders of New England as larger than life—larger, at least, than modern life. They were earnest, principled, courageous, and inspired. Even in their crimes they were magnificent. When De Forest compared the witchcraft delusion of the seventeenth century to the spiritualist delusion of the nineteenth, the latter looked tawdry. Calling spirit rappings and table turnings "meaningless" and "destitute of philosophy," he said that "the Salem witchcraft was comparatively a heroic affair; it was vitalized by a positive and fervent faith." As he surveyed the modern mind—scientific, skeptical, thoroughly prudent—he wondered if some precious capacities had not been lost: "Is humanity to be allowed no faith, no wonders? Witchcraft is gone; the devil and his angels are going; and animal magnetism is a poor substitute. Is the imagination to be spoiled utterly . . . ?" When the Puritans disappeared, they took with them the "faith" and "imagination" that lent grandeur to human life.[14]

Like other men of his time, De Forest was saddened by this loss; but unlike some of them, he was able to overcome his sadness. As long as it was merely a phase in the nostalgia syndrome, sadness was bound to be overborne by a renewed enthusiasm for the present and a rejection of the past. When he examined witching times, De Forest knew that faith and imagination were what had caused the execution of twenty people at Salem Village. He vividly revealed the unappealing side of Puritanism by depicting the torture of Giles Cory. Accused of being a wizard, Cory courageously refused to cooperate with the court by entering a plea. In response, the court ordered him pressed under a pile of rocks until he started talking. When he finally did talk, all he said was, "More weight!" Focusing on a gruesome detail reported by Robert Calef, De Forest portrayed the Puritans at their brutal worst. When the dying Cory's tongue jutted from his mouth, the sheriff used a cane to push it back in again. The "offensive horror" of superstition and cruelty outweighed the admiration the reader or the author had for faith and imagination. Early in the book, then again in the very last sentence, De Forest spelled out the "lesson" the story taught: "even in such a trinity as faith, hope, and charity, the greatest and most beautiful thing of all is charity."[15] Just as American morals were more important than European manners, so modern charity was more important than ancient faith.

Every exotic place was a breeding ground for nostalgia, not only Puritan New England but also the Orient. When De Forest visited the Holy Land, and when he wrote about it years later, he frequently yearned for days of old, when swords were bright and steeds were prancing. On a ship crowded with pilgrims bound for Jerusalem, he was reminded of the Crusaders who centuries earlier had ridden "a tide of enthusiasm" that carried them "through suffering and death to reach a fabled shrine." Sorrowfully he noted that "it would be hard now to find three hundred thousand spirits winged with a living poesy" and said that "the enthusiasm, self-devotion, and energy of the old crusaders soar loftily through my imagination." There was a grandeur about the past, a grandeur that mocked the humdrum business of modern times. This decline from the past to the present was apparent even in regard to "lovingness and loveliness." While traversing the Mediterranean, De Forest wondered why Mother Nature had stopped creating women like Helen of Troy and Cleopatra and why men no longer were possessed by "that love which for a woman would bury the halls of Troy in ashes and for a woman would fling away the empire of the earth." Nineteenth-century women, it seemed, did not drive men to such sublime folly. Something beautiful and something brave had passed from human life.

Despite the melancholy tone of this observation, however, De Forest remained a thoroughly modern man. After casting the usual wistful glances at the past and issuing the perfunctory sigh, he pointed out that Crusaders, Greeks, and Romans had exhibited grotesque stupidity and immorality. Regarding the Crusaders, he believed that their goal had been to secure possession of fraudulent shrines where superstitious pilgrims could engage in useless forms of worship. The "insignificant end of such a mighty endeavor," he said, "reposes in the quiet slough of my contempt." As for Helen and Cleopatra, De Forest knew that, although they were very pleasant in their way, they were not as proper as ladies ought to be. Few, indeed, of the ancient heroines could meet the exacting moral standards of Connecticut. After De Forest asked Mother Nature why she no longer produced such women, he received an answer that put the inquiry to an end: "'Peace!' replies Nature, 'the times that are are better than the times that have been; and the beauty of virtue is better than the beauty of vice. Since my youth I am growing ever wiser and juster; and I break every symbol, that I may gradually make place for reality.'" As a Yankee, De Forest knew instinctively that no face, however lovely, was worth a thousand ships. Thus, when he contemplated antiquity, he was thrilled by its "poesy" and symbolic truth but was disgusted by its squalid "reality." As usual, his excited imagination gave way to his forbidding judgment. Nostalgia ran its course.[16]

De Forest's attitude toward the past was epitomized by his attitude toward one of the most interesting activities of primitive peoples—torture. In his first two books, De Forest devoted considerable attention to this ritual—not only the torture of Giles Cory by the Puritans but also several acts of torture by the Indians of Connecticut. Oddly enough, even this phenomenon aroused in him a particle of nostalgia. One quality the Puritans and Indians possessed in abundance was courage, and in depicting scenes of torture, De Forest had the opportunity to show his admiration for this virtue. It was with utmost respect that he portrayed an Indian victim who, "with the flames shrivelling his skin, and the live coals scorching his flesh, sternly suppressed every sound or look which could betray his anguish, hurled back defiance in the face of his enemies, and shouted his war-song even while the hand of death was feeling for his heart-strings."[17] In the Indian warrior, De Forest saw a true romantic hero. The writer would later remark on the pitiful delicacy of modern men and their inability to endure pain. Civilization, alas, had vitiated their stamina and nerve.

But here again, De Forest would not let sentiment carry him too far. There were questions to be raised, after all, about the morality of people who burned others at the stake. The spectacle of a torture scene, he said,

> will not let us forget that, whatever of romance there may have been about the character and life of Indians, they were yet a race of unmitigated savages. . . . The spirit of the age is altogether adverse to barbarism, even when bedecked with all the feathers of imagination; and the sentimental eloquence of Rousseau, and other philosophers like him, is no longer sufficient to make men wish themselves savages.

The Indians of Connecticut thus received the same treatment from De Forest as had the Crusaders and the Puritans. They stirred his "imagination" by representing "romance"; but, finally, he repudiated them and chose godly decency over godlike heroism, the present over the past.[18]

Nostalgia means the pain of going home. When a grown man revisits the scenes of his childhood, he may be touched by memories and may yearn for what he, long ago, left behind. Still, he does not often wish to make his homecoming permanent; he does not want to move back in with Mom and Dad. So when J. W. De

Forest wrote about the past, revisiting the childhood of human civilization, his twinges of sentiment were not potent enough to make him want to abandon the modern age. However melancholy he might make himself by envisioning the lost decorum, faith, imagination, poetry, courage, and heroism of antiquity, he still could cheer himself by remembering the energy and integrity, rationality and humanity, of the nineteenth century. In the final reckoning, the quiet virtues of the present counted for more than the turbulent virtues of the past.

De Forest's victory over nostalgia was demonstrated not only by what he said but also by how he said it—his tone. Even when he lamented the loss of the past, he sometimes did so in such a way as to make that past seem unworthy of being missed. In *Seacliff,* for example, his apology for writing about everyday events sounded almost like a boast: "After all, is it my fault that I live in a degenerate age, when there are no dragons, nor enchanters, nor hardly any pirates, and when fathers do not immure their recusant daughters in sloppy dungeons?"[19] De Forest's irony punctured the bubble of nostalgia. As long as he could laugh at the past, he was in no danger of surrendering the present.

The speciousness of De Forest's paeans to "faith" and "poesy" was highlighted by his persistent debunking of these same qualities. In his travel books, for example, he avoided the sublime attractions of Europe and the Orient, devoting himself instead to ordinary sights, such as the costumes of peasants, and to ordinary experiences, such as fleeing from unemployed tour guides. In part, this restriction was because earlier travel writers had described, repeatedly and at length, all the romantic scenes; De Forest and other latecomers had to settle for what remained. Mostly, however, De Forest's concentration on the quotidian was a matter of preference. He mocked writers who saw traces of glory everywhere, considering them soft-minded victims of conventional delusions, and gladly attended to reality instead:

> And here I might outpour an endless prattle
> About high art, and scenery, and song,
> Or heroes' graves, or fields of ancient battle,

Or broken fanes which to old gods belong;
But I shall not; my forte is tittle-tattle
Concerning living men, the motley throng
Which greets the tourist's lazy observation
In street, and shop, and coach, and railway station.

Talk of high art and heroes and old gods and antiquity was "prattle"; a serious writer wrote of living men. J. W. De Forest was serious.[20]

Chapter 4

A friend of ours . . . has the craze in his head that he will some day write a great American novel.

J. W. De Forest, "The Great American Novel," 1868

The Civil War thrust Americans into strange new roles. The war turned slaves into free people, provincial Yankees into nationalists, and J. W. De Forest into an infantry officer. In the 1850s, De Forest had been writing novels and stories, traveling, leading the delicate life of the sophisticated modern. Often his thoughts had turned back to earlier centuries when roughnecks like the Romans and the Indians trod the earth, and sometimes he had indulged in nostalgic fantasies about primitive ways of life. Now, though, the outbreak of war put a saber in his hand and enabled him actually to live the hard life of the ancients. It was as if he had fallen into the midst of his dream.

That experience changed him in three different but related ways. First, it strengthened his admiration for the martial virtues; as a soldier, he learned to place an even higher value on courage, discipline, and fortitude than he had done when he was a historian who wrote about soldiers. Second, it strengthened his self-regard, for he himself demonstrated those martial virtues during the war. Third, by strengthening his self-regard, it strengthened his insistence on doing what he felt like doing, namely writing. As a combat veteran, he did not have to worry about seeming effete; as a man who had helped to save the Union and free the slaves, he did not need to feel useless. Now, with a clean conscience, he could spend all day at a writing desk.

He also became a tolerably happy man. During these years, De Forest felt more satisfaction not only with himself but also with his country and his time than he had ever felt before. In the 1850s, his delight in modern rationality had been slightly diminished by his nostalgia over the loss of ancient wildness and romance. But now—at Gettysburg and Chickamauga and even at Cedar Creek—men were showing that civilization need not be accompanied by decadence, that even Yankees, the most up-to-date of men, could still be heroes in the ancient fashion. Glory had not vanished from the earth along with the Founding Fathers. It was still available for De Forest and his generation to share.

In 1860–1861, Dr. Charles Shepard was spending the winter in Charleston, as was his custom. He had taken his daughter Fanny with him; but, this time, daughter Harriet stayed in New Haven with her husband—until the secession crisis. On January 16, 1861, four weeks after a South Carolina convention voted to withdraw from the Union, Harriet and J. W. De Forest boarded a steamer headed for the heart of the rebellion. They may have gone south to assist Dr. Shepard, who, despite his fifty-six years of age, had been ordered to take his turn patrolling the streets at night. In addition, however, they wanted to see how the rebellion was progressing. De Forest, whose career as a novelist seemed to have reached a dead end, was exploring the possibility of a career as a journalist. While rejoining his father-in-law, he took the opportunity to investigate "Charleston under Arms." In an article published in the *Atlantic* just as the war broke out, De Forest proved himself sympathetically critical of the rebels.[1]

The secessionists, he said, were motivated by an unfounded but understandable fear that, unless the Union were dissolved, Northern antislavery people would provoke a slave uprising in the South. Having witnessed the surliness of the bondsmen, De Forest shared the white Southerners' dread of insurrection and, therefore, could sympathize with their abhorrence of any Northern policy or sentiment that might even *seem* to encourage an uprising: "If you live in a powder-magazine [he said], you positively must feel inhospitably inclined toward a man who presents himself with a cigar in his mouth. Even if he shows you that it is but a fireless stump, it still makes you uneasy." De Forest, who like many Yankees was as hostile to immediate abolition as to slavery itself, believed that the North would not in fact stimulate black revolution, but he understood white Southerners' anxieties well enough not to blame secession on any failing worse than ignorance and fear. He hesitated to call a disunionist a traitor, for the man was only doing what he thought was right.[2]

After about ten days in Charleston, the De Forests accompanied the Shepards on their return to the North. De Forest's whereabouts for the next five months are uncertain, but by June he was in New England.[3] Meanwhile, much was happening in the South. In April the rebels seized Fort Sumter, and in July they humiliated the Union army at Bull Run. The outbreak of bloodshed provoked a little civil war in the De Forest household. The females—Harriet, her sister Fanny, and Louis's nurse Mary—all favored the Confederacy. The males—John, Dr. Shepard, Harriet's brother Charles Jr., and Rev. Shepard—all were for the Union. Rev. Shepard lamented that the family included "traitors, pro-slavery secessionists who rejoice in the successes of the enemy." Paraphrasing either Abraham Lincoln or the Gospel According to St. Mark, he reported that "the house is divided & the discussions are lively." This liveliness, like the wailing of small children, was probably of the sort that J. W. De Forest could do without.[4]

While his wife rejoiced over Confederate victories, De Forest joined the Union army. By October 1861 he had "made up his mind to go to the war" (as one of his in-laws reported) and was "all engaged" in recruiting a company of volunteers. Following the custom of the nineteenth-century army, De Forest's commissioning as an officer of volunteers depended on his enrolling enough men to serve under him. He therefore worked hard at recruiting, setting up an office in New Haven and traveling to nearby cities such as Bridgeport. After a few weeks of such exertion, he began to lose weight. "He finds the getting up of a Company hard labor, after four or five years of idleness," commented Rev. Shepard."It will do him good." Since De Forest had little contact with rank and file citizens, he resorted to the newspapers to spur enlistments. The *New Haven Journal and Courier* and the *Palladium* carried advertisements for his company, which he had named the Putnam Guards (after Gen. Israel Putnam, Connecticut's Revolutionary War hero). The new outfit, said the announcement, would be "of the first class, both physically and morally. No pains will be spared by its officers to make it the crack Company of the regiment, both in its choice of men and the thoroughness of discipline." In an accompanying editorial, the *Journal and Courier* added that Captain De Forest was "a gentleman of the very highest character."[5]

The Putnam Guards were to be part of the Twelfth Regiment of Connecticut Volunteers, the "Charter Oak Regiment," which was being organized as an elite corps in the New England Division. By touting the Putnam Guards as the crack company in that regiment, De Forest showed that he intended to make his command the crème de la crème. However, it did not work out that way. Like other recruiters in the Twelfth, he found that men did not flock to units that prided themselves on the thoroughness of their discipline and the gentlemanly quality of their officers. Instead, the recruits signed up under commanders who had proved themselves good companions in the past; men of the common sort who were not averse to bending an ear or an elbow with men who were now their subordinates. De Forest recalled his own experience when, in *Miss Ravenel's Conversion,* he described Captain Colburne's difficulty finding volunteers: "Not having belonged to a fire company or militia company, nor even kept a bar or billiard-saloon, he had no retainers nor partisans nor shopmates to call upon, no rummy customers whom he could engage in the war-dance on condition of unlimited whiskey." Like Colburne, De Forest spent much time alone in his recruiting office, as did many officers of the high-toned Charter Oak Regiment. A month after publishing De Forest's advertisement for volunteers, the *Journal and Courier* derided the Twelfth as "going the way of all fancy Regiments. . . . It was puffed into notoriety, and was expected to be a favorite, . . . but it amounts to nothing more than any other." Facing competition from other recruiters in New Haven, De Forest could fill the ranks of his company only by offering extra bounties.[6]

Even with the added inducements, enlistment went slowly. When he finally reached his quota, he found that he was the ninth company commander to do so. His company was thus denominated by the letter I, ninth in the alphabet, and De Forest was the regiment's ninth captain in order of seniority. This ranking proved important to his career, since promotion within the regiment depended largely on length of service. With eight captains ahead of him, De Forest could not easily move up.[7]

The seniority system worked powerfully against his advancement, but De Forest also found a second huge obstacle—politics. In 1863, for example, when the regiment's major was severely wounded, De Forest did not expect to be named his replacement. If the majority were to become vacant, he said, the colonel would probably recommend "some brother tinker, or the Governor would see a chance to buy another democrat."[8] Since he believed that the saloon keeper's social status and the political boss's ability to deliver votes were the twin requisites for preferment, De Forest felt that the army discriminated against gentlemen. In 1864 the regiment's senior captain was elevated to major, a promotion apparently based on seniority, not politics. Still, De Forest was not satisfied. He did not comment on the new major's military competence but observed that he was a joiner by trade. In 1863 De Forest told his brother that a bright and brave private named Skinner had no chance to rise because he was under the command of "an ignorant low-bred captain who does not know what a gentleman is, & if he did, would dislike the same." Because Skinner would not "flatter a boor," he stood no chance of promotion.[9]

Though De Forest deplored the presumed political character of military appointments, he was not above using what little influence he had. In 1862 he asked his wife to solicit "influential persons" for letters urging his promotion. Harriet did so and sent the letters to the governor, but her husband still got no promotion. De Forest cannot thus be said to have scorned all politicking in the military, only that that might result in the advancement of boors.[10]

De Forest did have one opportunity for promotion. While stationed in New Orleans in 1862, he was offered (unofficially) the colonelcy of one of the black regiments being organized by Benjamin Butler. De Forest declined—a decision he later would sometimes regret. In 1864, by which time he realized the hopelessness of advancement within his old regiment, he explained to Andrew De Forest that he had refused the colonelcy because such positions had been in "bad odor" for two reasons. First, the government had not yet sanctioned the raising of black troops, and it would have been foolish to give up a captaincy for a colonelcy that might never exist. Second, Butler had placed men of "exceedingly bad character" in command of the black regiments, and De Forest would have lost prestige by being associated with such officers. In later years, De Forest repeated these two explanations and added two more. In *A Volunteer's Adventures,* he said that, when offered the promotion, he had believed that black troops would be put to work building roads and bridges and draining marshes—not fighting—and thus would give their commander "small chance for distinction." Moreover, though facing little danger from combat, they would suffer much from climate and disease since they would be used to garrison the least healthful positions in the South. All in all, De Forest had concluded, it was better to be a captain of whites than a colonel of blacks.[11]

De Forest received his commission in January 1862; in late February his regiment was shipped south. After waiting out the conquest of New Orleans, the Twelfth Connecticut took part in the occupation of the city. In October 1862, De Forest came under fire for the first time, while pursuing Confederate forces through the swamps of Louisiana. In May and June 1863, he took part in the siege of Port Hudson, spending some forty days and nights in the trenches and joining in three storming parties. In late January 1864, a weary Captain De Forest went home on furlough, but in mid-April he returned to Louisiana. Soon thereafter, his regiment marched north to help defend Washington from Jubal Early, and De Forest participated in the battles of Winchester, Fisher's Hill, and Cedar Creek.[12]

De Forest's wartime experiences strengthened his respect for the martial virtues and reinforced his assurance that he possessed them. In *History of the Indians,* he had admired a warrior's ability to withstand torture, and in *European Acquaintance* he had prided himself on enduring the bone-chilling rigors of *Kaltwasserkur.* But the Civil War gave De Forest the opportunity to rise from mock-heroism to the real thing. Instead of cold baths and bland food, he now faced bullets, disease, and genuine hunger. Though he had always praised masculinity, he now had the opportunity to prove himself a man.

From the beginning, he was aware that he was undergoing a test of valor. On the troop ship steaming south in March 1862, he wrote a letter to his wife in which he assured her that the tremulousness of his handwriting was due to the shaking of the ship's engine, not to any personal trepidation. Before going into battle for the first time, he worried that his men would disgrace him by running away or, worse, that he would disgrace himself; but, according to his own published accounts, he did not worry much about getting killed—he feared death less than humiliation. In *A Volunteer's Adventures,* he recalled experiencing moments of dread during an attack on Port Hudson and during the Battle of Cedar Creek, but he recalled these moments as "ridiculous and contemptible." At the Battle of Fisher's Hill, he ordered his men to shoot down a bluecoat who was fleeing the field.[13]

While touring Europe a decade earlier, De Forest had despised Florentine dandies for being "rather effeminate" and had worried that wearing a nosegay in his buttonhole might make himself seem "a most lackadaisical trifler." During the war, De Forest purged himself of any doubts of his ruggedness. "What with starving, freezing, swamp fever, forced marches, and being shot," he said, "war is glorious fun." Sleeping in the field with just his blanket and a coverlet over him, he looked with contempt upon his rheumatic tentmate who slept on "a bedsack stuffed with cornhusks, which looks effeminate." After two years of being "cold & hungry & unsheltered," De Forest learned to "draw a broad distinction between the words discomfort and suffering." Constant deprivation, he began to believe, did not make one wretched, for one could get used to anything. "We waste unnecessary sympathy," he concluded, "on poor people." As if to show his own habituated toughness, he did not even mention it to his wife when he received a slight bullet wound, which he dismissed as "a scratch on the shin." The war came as a blessing to a scribbler, a perpetual vacationer, who had often worried about seeming "effeminate." After serving in the infantry, De Forest no longer needed to fear comparison with his father, his brothers, or any other active, productive men of the world. From the businessman's perspective, the novelist had looked effete; but now, from the soldier's point of view, the businessman himself seemed to be wearing skirts.[14]

Like others of his time, De Forest imagined the Civil War as a fiery trial that purged America of materialism and returned the nation to the heroic idealism that had ennobled the past. However much De Forest in the 1850s had deplored the "fanaticism" of Puritans and Crusaders and Greeks, he had always admired their selflessness. However irrational or cruel the ancients had been, they had also been courageous enough to fling away their lives and fortunes for a cause—whether a shrine in the Levant, a tenet of Reformed theology, or the retrieval of Helen of Troy. Modern men, in contrast, had seemed devoted only to filling their pockets and their bellies. In his nostalgic moods, De Forest had bemoaned the fact that "faith" and "enthusiasm" had given way to a cautious, acquisitive self-indulgence. But the war seemed to change all that. As Northerners by the hundreds of thousands risked or sacrificed their lives for things as mysterious as the Union or (in some cases) equality, De Forest interpreted this sacrifice as a glorious overcoming of Yankee materialism. In a novel, he called Bull Run a "blessing in disguise"; and in a poem, he said that the suffering incurred at that debacle had cleansed the North of selfishness:

> O comrades, render thanks to God
> For Bull Run's day of panic terrors.

That overthrow was Yahveh's rod
To scourge afar the groveling errors
That trade is mankind's loftiest pride
And man's most precious part, his hide.[15]

The war provided De Forest with a heroic standard against which he could judge all subsequent history. From 1862 to 1864 he felt certain, for the first and last time, that he was doing good work in a good cause. He would later look back on the Civil War as a high point in his career and the nation's. Remembering the *pum* of distant cannons, the whiz of musketry, the groans of wounded men, and the shouts of the victorious, De Forest observed, "almost with a feeling of sadness," that he would never be in battle again. Instead, he knew, he would busy himself with the commonplace: elections, commerce, social calls, church going. In nostalgic retrospect, the war seemed to symbolize sacrifice and glory, and for the rest of his life he would look back fondly on that golden time.[16]

But on December 2, 1864, De Forest left the army. In September of that year he had told his brother of his intention to be mustered out and had specified two reasons: he believed (correctly) that the war was nearly over, and he was "getting somewhat disgusted with these continual privations."[17] Danger and suffering were fine experiences to remember in comfortable afteryears, but they did not have quite so much appeal to a soldier in the field. In 1851 De Forest had left the "savage" water cure at Graefenberg for the more "effeminate" one at Divonne; in 1864 he left the army for civilian life. In both decisions, he chose the more comfortable course, but in both he admired (in retrospect) the more severe.

For De Forest the Civil War was a disappointment in only one way: it had not afforded him much opportunity for distinction. For months he was stationed in Louisiana without seeing combat. Wishing that he were on the Potomac or the Rappahannock instead, he complained that nobody was getting killed, so nobody had a chance for promotion. Later he did get into battles, but they were not quite big enough to draw the eyes of the world upon him. The Shenandoah Valley campaign of 1864 made a hero of Philip Sheridan and contributed to the fame of George Custer and Rutherford B. Hayes; but it was no Gettysburg. Like Captain Colburne of *Miss Ravenel's Conversion*, who longed to take part in "the great battle of the war," De Forest was doomed to be stationed on the fringes of history. He served with competence and courage, but he did not win fame. It may have rankled when he noted that his brigade commander, General Godfrey Weitzel, was a decade younger than himself; and it may have been with envy that Captain De Forest reported another general's admiring comment that the "young man" Philip Sheridan had already "made a great name for himself." De Forest, five years older than Sheridan, left the army at the same rank at which he had entered it three long years before.[18]

He also left it a sick man. While in the field proving his toughness, he had contracted a disease (probably dysentery) that gave him chronic diarrhea. When he returned to New Haven in January 1865, he was thin and his ankles were swollen. The seriousness of his illness was noted by Rev. Shepard: "Mrs. De Forest was in & says Mr. De Forest is no better & growing worse. If he has strength to stand against the disease why he will get well [;] if not he will die. She is very resigned to what God appoints." De Forest himself was rather less resigned. He underwent homeopathic medical treatment, and he sought to regain strength by eating plenty of food, especially rare beef. Rev. Shepard thought such a diet was a strange remedy for diarrhea, but apparently it worked. De Forest was soon going out with his wife to hear Wendell Phillips lecture on "The Spirit of the Times" and was going out by himself for a night with the boys.[19]

He also was writing fiction again. Back in 1859, De Forest had "caved in" on being a novelist and had begun to settle into the role of a journalist. During the war, he had continued in that role, publishing battle reports in *Harper's*; but he had also produced at least one short story, "Doctor Hawley," published in 1863. Now, back in New Haven, he was hard at work on the novel *Miss Ravenel's Conversion*. Military service, it seems, had resuscitated De Forest's literary ambitions. The army had provided him with a steady salary to support his family and also with sufficient leisure time to write. The war had given him a subject worth writing about, had supplied him with the material for many of his most enduring works. Serving honorably in sieges and storming parties had strengthened his self-confidence so that he no longer felt useless or effete because he was a writer. The United States Army had saved De Forest's career as a novelist. It would continue to help him, even when the war was over.

In April 1865, just a few days before Lee's surrender at Appomattox, Rev. Shepard reported that De Forest was "very well & keeps *busy* writing a *killing* novel! I hope it will not kill the writer pecuniarily, but fear." The writer himself seems to have shared that fear. Realizing that military pay was more reliable than payments from publishers, he had applied for another commission as an officer; and in May he finally received it. Because of his "army sickness," he was eligible to join the Veteran Reserve Corps (formerly named the Invalid Corps), whose purpose was to supply partially disabled veterans for administrative, garrison, and police duties in order to free able-bodied men for field duty. In the summer of 1865, De Forest returned to uniform (again as a captain) and traveled to Washington (again leaving his family behind). One of his main assignments was to write a history of the Veteran Reserve Corps to justify its continued existence now that the war was over. In this regard, he seems to have failed: at General Grant's insistence, the corps was disbanded in July 1866.[20]

De Forest managed to stay in the army, however, by transferring to the Bureau of Refugees, Freedmen, and Abandoned Lands. Like some other agents in the bureau, he was motivated less by a desire to serve the freedmen than by a desire to receive a government salary. He even got a promotion to brevet major, the only military advancement he would ever receive. After spending a furlough with his wife and child in Connecticut (the first such visit in over a year), he took a steamer to Charleston, where he was to become the Freedmen's Bureau adjutant general for South Carolina. Mrs. De Forest was to join him later in the year.[21]

Fickle Fortune, however, intervened. When Major De Forest arrived in Charleston in September 1866, he found that South Carolina *already* had an adjutant general of the Freedmen's Bureau, a man who had no intention of giving up his post. De Forest, as the newcomer, was relegated to the lowly position of district commander in the northwest corner of the state. His headquarters was at Greenville, some fourteen hours by railroad from Charleston, and fourteen hours might as well have been a thousand. Mrs. De Forest and Louis continued living in New Haven, made at least one trip to Charleston along with Dr. Shepard, but, so far as is known, never visited Greenville.[22]

Arriving at his outpost in October 1866, De Forest spent the next fifteen months overseeing about forty thousand whites and twenty thousand blacks in Greenville, Pickens, and Anderson counties. The work was seldom strenuous. Usually spending only three to five hours of "labor or lounging" in his office each day, he had plenty of time for writing. De Forest, nevertheless, took his task as a bureau officer seriously. Wishing to give the South a genuine reconstruction, he sought to develop in the region's inhabitants those virtues he believed predominant in the North, particularly a respect for law.[23]

His "first and great duty," De Forest believed, "lay in raising the blacks and restoring the whites of my district to a confidence in civil law, thus fitting both as rapidly as possible to assume the duties of citizenship." Reluctant to use troops to secure order and justice, the Yankee major hoped the Southerners would discipline themselves. If punishment were inflicted by an alien military force, he thought, the people would never learn the art of self-government. Thus, when a Carolinian yelled to him, "God damn your Yankee soul to hell," De Forest did not arrest the man but asked the civil authorities to look into the matter. Similarly, when a former slave named Cato Allums killed one of six whites who tried to force their way into his home, De Forest did not offer Allums military protection but instead urged him to submit to arrest and trial by local magistrates in Pickens district on charges of murder. There is no record of what happened to the man who hollered insults at De Forest, but Cato Allums was eventually released from custody. De Forest interpreted this latter action as a sign that blacks could receive justice from Carolina courts and that white Southerners, at least in his district, were "amenable to reason and considerate in sentiment." The head of the Freedmen's Bureau in South Carolina had asked his subordinates to inform him of racial discrimination in the state courts so that he might intervene on behalf of blacks. Some agents did report such irregularities, but De Forest found none. As he told one of his superiors, "Legally the negro is accepted as the equal of the white man."[24]

Not all the evidence, however, supports this optimistic conclusion. Cato Allums submitted to arrest partly to avoid lynching by the angry white citizens of Pickens. He was freed on bail only after his five surviving assailants left the state without testifying against him—and at least a month after the district solicitor had ordered his release. He had to pay various costs for his defense, the five whites were never arrested, and Allums found it advisable to move to Tennessee for a year. Other events in De Forest's corner of South Carolina also indicated that the scales of justice were imperfectly balanced. There was, for example, one case so notorious that it was the subject of a ninety-eight page report by the Department of War.[25]

One night in October 1867 the blacks of Pickens district were meeting at a private house to organize a chapter of the Union League (also known as the Loyal League), whose purpose was to involve blacks in politics, specifically Republican Party politics. Having received threats of violence, they had posted sentries around the house. Violence came—in the stumbling, palefaced form of a sometime hog thief named Bob Smith. Fortified by whiskey, Smith fired a pistol ball into the wall of the Union League building, then fled to a nearby school, where a debate was being held, and took refuge behind a group of white men and boys in the yard. When several league sentries arrived and tried to seize Smith, the whites resisted and a scuffle broke out. A pistol was fired, and a fourteen-year-old boy named Miles Hunnicutt fell with a fatal wound in the back of the neck. The blacks claimed that Smith, standing behind Hunnicutt, had done the shooting;

the whites claimed that Hunnicutt had turned to run and had been shot from behind by one of the blacks. The civil government of Pickens filed charges against nine blacks plus Alexander Bryce Jr., the sole white man who had attended the Union League meeting. At the end of the trial, Bryce and three of the blacks were acquitted; a black named December Gadsden, the sergeant of the guard, was found guilty of shooting Hunnicutt; the five remaining sentries were found guilty of aiding and abetting Gadsden; and all six convicted men were sentenced to be hanged. A few days before the executions were to be carried out, however, the governor of South Carolina and a United States marshal interrogated the condemned men, and one of the latter accused another, Nat Frazier, of having pulled the trigger. Frazier, under further interrogation, confessed. The governor then commuted the sentences of Gadsden and the other four sentries to prison terms ranging from two to five years; only Frazier was hanged. As for Bob Smith, the man who started it all, he was convicted some months later by a military court in Charleston on charges of malicious mischief, discharging a firearm in the nighttime, and carrying a deadly weapon and was sentenced to six months at hard labor. Noting that civil authorities had prosecuted Union League members but not the man who had shot at them, an army investigator said that Bob Smith deserved to be punished: "It is to be regretted that he was not indicted and put on trial with the other rioters."[26]

The judicial proceedings in this case are remarkable in two ways. First, it is apparent that the death sentences ordered for the six sentries were used to frighten them into talking. Although it took less than two weeks to arrest, try, convict, and sentence the men, their execution was put off for more than a month— long enough for them to brood on the fact that it was not necessary for all of them to die. If one would confess, the others would be spared. It is possible that Nat Frazier confessed merely to save his friends. Second, it should be remembered that the jury had ruled that December Gadsden had fired the pistol and that Frazier had merely been one of five men who had aided and abetted him. Later, however, the magistrate decided that the roles had been reversed, that Frazier had been the killer and that he alone must pay with his life. To a skeptical observer it might seem as if it did not really matter who was hanged, just as long as he was black.

J. W. De Forest, however, was not a skeptical observer. Indeed, he was not an observer at all. Although Pickens was one of the districts for which he was responsible, the bureau major made it a policy never to leave his headquarters in Greenville. Consequently, he took no part in the murder trial, and he seems to have relied on hearsay as his source of information rather than on pretrial depositions or courtroom testimony. In October 1868, he published an article in the *Atlantic* that somewhat misrepresented the facts of the case. He said, for example, that Bob Smith claimed to have approached the Union League meeting by mistake; in actuality, however, Smith testified that he never went near the meeting. De Forest reported that eight men were sentenced to death for Miles Hunnicutt's killing; actually six were. He mentioned the confession of Nat Frazier but did not question the means by which it was obtained. Most important, De Forest did not report the blacks' assertion that Hunnicutt was shot in the back of the neck because a drunken and terrified Bob Smith was blazing away behind him. De Forest, then, was short on facts. This deficiency, however, did not prevent him from drawing large generalizations about freedmen like Frazier and scalawags like Alexander Bryce. "This affair was mainly important as showing how easily the Negroes could be led into folly and crime," he told the readers of the *Atlantic*. "Themselves a peaceful race, not disposed to rioting and murder, they were brought without trouble to both by the counsels of the ignorant and pugnacious whites who became their leaders in the Loyal Leagues." Such were the convictions of a man entrusted with the reconstruction of race relations in South Carolina.[27]

During his fifteen months in Greenville, De Forest probably paid less attention to the fate of Bob Smith or Cato Allums than to that of a young lady named Lillie Ravenel. He had begun *Miss Ravenel's Conversion,* a novel of the Civil War, late in 1864 and had sold it to Harpers in 1865. The novel (analyzed in chapter 5) involved three major characters whose real-life prototypes were obvious: Lillie Ravenel, a Northern woman of Southern principles like Harriet Shepard De Forest; Dr. Ravenel, Lillie's father, a mineralogist like Dr. Shepard; and Edward Colburne, a bookish young man who, like De Forest, becomes a captain in the Union army. The novel also includes major characters whose prototypes, if any, had best not be revealed: the seductive Madame Larue and the all-too-seducible Colonel John Carter.[28]

The House of Harpers had originally intended to publish the novel serially in *Harper's New Monthly Magazine,* then to reissue it as a book. After having second thoughts about the effect on morally sensitive readers of the novel's episode of adultery and smattering of obscenities, Harpers proposed what De Forest called the "moral reform of the story." In December 1865, the author told his editor that he did not object to such censorship but added that "I think it ought to be understood, for the sake of *vraisemblance,* that the Colonel did frequently swear & that the Louisiana lady was not quite as good as she should be." Harpers apparently yielded on this point, for in the published novel Colonel Carter and Madame Larue were not "reformed." However, Harpers also decided to spare many readers' delicate sensibilities by publishing *Miss Ravenel's Conversion* only in book form, not in a "family" magazine. This decision, to which De Forest assented soon after arriving in Greenville, must have disappointed him. Publication in *Harper's* would have brought him wide recognition and, in addition, would probably have stimulated the sale of the book.[29]

In May 1867, *Miss Ravenel's Conversion* finally appeared, and De Forest was in for another disappointment, one guaranteed to gall any fastidious writer. Because he was ensconced in Greenville, he had not been sent galley proofs from New York, and he had assumed that his editor would make any necessary corrections. He had assumed wrongly. When the book came out, it was deformed by more than a hundred printer's errors. Letters were broken, u's and n's interchanged, quotation marks omitted. *Haven't* was spelled in three different ways, and on page 45 Lillie

Ravenel was transformed into Libbie. It must have been apparent to De Forest that rather more craftsmanship had gone into the writing of the novel than into its publishing. Two decades later he recalled that the plates for *Miss Ravenel's Conversion* were almost the sloppiest he had ever seen.[30]

Reviews of the novel were mixed, but in favorable proportions. The *Atlantic* and *Harper's Weekly* praised it, placing special emphasis on the credibility of its characters. The *Nation,* however, disagreed, finding the characterization weak and pronouncing the book a "poor novel." Such criticism, however wrong-headed, may have distressed De Forest less than some of the praise he received. *Harper's New Monthly* applauded *Miss Ravenel's Conversion* for its plot, characterization, and style, then went on to call it "the best American novel published for many a year." De Forest may have devoted a bitter moment to contemplating the fact that *Harper's* had refused to serialize the best novel for many a year. It may have galled him even more that, from the fiscal point of view, the editors had made the right decision. The public, it seems, was not ready for *Miss Ravenel's Conversion.* When published as a book, the novel did not sell; hundreds of copies remained in a warehouse for decades; no second edition appeared in De Forest's lifetime; the printer's errors would go uncorrected.[31]

The sales record of this book was not De Forest's only frustration at this time. Shortly after publishing *Miss Ravenel's Conversion,* he completed another novel, seventy chapters long, that he titled "The Senator: a Romance." In March 1867, he reported that the manuscript had been "stolen" on its way from Charleston to New York, apparently en route to a publisher. This copy seems to have been the only one De Forest had, for he tried desperately to get it back. He wrote to a magazine editor, asking him to keep an eye out for the manuscript, and he took out a copyright on the book's title—all to no avail. He never published "The Senator," though he may have mined it for ideas for the political novels he produced in the 1870s. At best, the book was a partial loss.[32]

Despite these disappointments, De Forest kept writing. While in Greenville, he published four short stories, two of which dealt with Reconstruction themes, but none of which constituted a distinguished work of prose. "'Rum Creeters is Women,'" for example, offered insights such as, "It is better and holier to love than it is to hate." Far more original and memorable than these stories were De Forest's nonfiction essays in literary and social criticism. It was probably during his last months with the Freedmen's Bureau that he composed three of his best short works: "The Great American Novel," a critique of current fiction; "Two Girls," a comparison of the old-fashioned and the modern; and "The 'High-Toned Gentleman,'" a critical appreciation of the Southern cavalier.[33]

When De Forest was not busy writing articles or stories, he was writing letters to extract payment for them. Trying to support a wife and child on a genteel plane of existence, he always had to wring every possible cent from his publishers. When in 1867 the *Galaxy* paid him only forty dollars for a fourteen-page story, De Forest protested. "It is too little," he said. "I am not a new beginner, nor do I think that I am yet worn out." Confident of the quality of his work, he said that if he did not receive five dollars a page, he would "send my wares to other merchants." His boldness paid off, for the magazine sent him an additional thirty dollars. By this time, De Forest was accustomed to haggling over prices—"You are probably quite as used to receiving such letters," he told the editors, "as I am to writing them"—and in the coming years he was to get even more such experience. In 1868, for example, he informed the *Galaxy* editors that they would have to raise their rates to match those of *Harper's*; in 1869 he told them that in order to keep up with the *Atlantic*, they would have to pay a hundred dollars per story. Besides good money, De Forest demanded prompt remuneration. Insisting on payment as soon as the piece was accepted, the author explained that "I shall seriously need the money."[34]

Though he would dicker over prices, De Forest did not enjoy the sport. "Excuse my business like style," he told editors. "I am . . . so light in purse as to feel no shame at bargaining." As a gentleman, De Forest had a prejudice against the "business like style," but, alas, he was often "light in purse." According to his son, he was "always hard pressed—in some years desperately so." He thus found himself in the most ungentlemanly position of constantly having to wheedle, threaten, and goad.[35]

By the end of 1867, De Forest confronted another crucial decision in his career. The Freedmen's Bureau was ordering its agents to begin traveling more frequently throughout their districts, settling each problem in the locale where it arose. If De Forest were to stay with the bureau, he would have to work more and write less. Moreover, the bureau was scheduled to be terminated in the summer of 1868, and the number of employees was already being cut back. (As it turned out, the force in South Carolina fell from eighty-eight in 1867 to nine in 1869.) Faced with this prospect, De Forest looked into alternatives. He considered running for Congress in South Carolina (on the "nigger vote," as Rev. Shepard phrased it); more than a tenth of the Freedmen's Bureau officials in South Carolina later went into politics in the state. Harriet, however, opposed such a move, and De Forest ultimately agreed with her. Instead he decided upon a course of action that would leave him plenty of opportunity to write and would not involve him in less congenial obligations. He decided to become a full-time, professional writer.[36]

This decision was audacious. Although De Forest may still have been drawing dividends from investments (there is no record concerning this), his income could not have been large enough to support his family in the style they expected. For years he had been saying that a man should never devote himself to writing unless he already had a comfortable income from some other source. Now, however, as he quit the Freedmen's Bureau and gave up his government salary, he was ignoring his own advice. Having endured the horrors of Port Hudson, he was ready to face the hard and precarious life of a literary free lance.[37]

An article he published his first month after leaving the army suggested why he had taken such a dangerous step. In "The Great American Novel," he described "a friend of ours"—obviously De Forest himself—who had served in the Civil War and in Reconstruction, had published several works well spoken of by critics but ignored by the public, and had written "articles and other things which he calls trivialities." Now, however, the "friend" wished to attempt something less trivial. Though "a fairly clever person, and by no means lacking in common sense on common subjects," he had "the craze in his head that he will some day write a great American novel."[38] So there it was. De Forest, now in his forties, was prepared at last to abandon prudence and to indulge crazy ideas. He was ready to undertake something heroic, something great.

Chapter 5

The democratic North means equality— every man standing on his own legs.

J. W. De Forest, *Miss Ravenel's Conversion*, 1867

From 1864, the year he left the Twelfth Connecticut Volunteers, to 1868, the year he left the Freedmen's Bureau, J. W. De Forest published the writings that would gain him a place in history. In 1864 *Harper's New Monthly* began issuing his series of battle reports: "The First Time Under Fire," "Sheridan's Battle of Winchester," "Sheridan's Victory of Middletown," and "Port Hudson." In 1867 De Forest's best book, *Miss Ravenel's Conversion,* appeared. In 1868 the *Nation* published two of De Forest's most influential essays, "The Great American Novel" and "The 'High-Toned Gentleman.'" In that same year, the *Galaxy* published "Forced Marches," the last of De Forest's articles about the Civil War, and various magazines issued his articles on Reconstruction: "The Low-Down People," "The Man and Brother," "A Bureau Major's Business and Pleasures," "A Report of Outrages," and "Chivalrous and Semi-Chivalrous Southrons." Some eighty years later, the Civil War and Reconstruction articles were collected, edited, and issued as books by the Yale University Press. These volumes, *A Volunteer's Adventures* and *A Union Officer in the Reconstruction,* have been frequently used and highly praised by historians. The years from 1864 to 1868 thus constituted De Forest's "major phase"—a phase as productive as it was brief.

Like his earlier works, those of the 1860s contrasted the present with the past. The past had previously been represented by

Europe and the Orient; now it was represented by the Old South. As before, De Forest found much to admire in the ancient way of life: bravery, chivalry, manners; and, as before, he found even more to despise: slavery and indolence and poverty, pugnacity and willful imbecility. It was the nostalgia syndrome all over again; and once again, De Forest, after a longing look at the past, resolutely turned about-face. Affirming his continued loyalty to the present, which he now associated with the Union, he made use of the character Dr. Ravenel to sum up the meaning of the Civil War:

> "The victory of the North [says Ravenel] is at bottom the triumph of laboring men living by their own industry, over non-laboring men who wanted to live by the industry of others. . . . The pro-slavery South meant oligarchy and imitated the manners of the European nobility. The democratic North means equality—every man standing on his own legs and not bestriding other men's shoulders—every man passing for just what he is and no more. It means honesty, sincerity, frankness in word as well as deed. It means general hard work, too, in consequence of which there is less chance to cultivate the graces."[1]

Industry, self-reliance, and honesty were familiar items in the list of modern virtues De Forest had compiled in the 1850s. He had found them lacking in Europe and the Levant but wonderfully abundant in the United States. He now merely refined his analysis and ascribed them only to the states north of the Mason-Dixon line. But one virtue Dr. Ravenel mentions—equality—had not previously been emphasized by De Forest. Hitherto, he had paid little attention to the notion that all men are created equal. Now, however, as he took up arms in a war on behalf of precisely that proposition, this proud gentleman of Whiggish family found himself penning the praises of the common man. De Forest never entirely shook off his aristocratic prejudices, but between 1864 and 1868 he came as close as he ever would. The happy result was *Miss Ravenel's Conversion*.

The finest product of the Old South—the emblem and epitome of that alien culture—was what De Forest called the "high-toned gentleman" or the "chivalrous Southron." In Dixie's aristocracy, the Yankee discovered many of the same admirable characteristics he had previously found in the Crusaders, the Indians, the Puritans, and the European nobility. They were "more simple than we," he said, "more provincial, more antique, more picturesque," and they had more of "the primitive, the natural virtues." These strange creatures of the past who had somehow survived into modern times were destined for rapid extinction. But before they disappeared, said De Forest, Northerners ought to study them and "engraft upon ourselves" their "nobler qualities."[2]

De Forest identified at least three such qualities. First, the high-toned gentleman had "a fine self-respect." Possessing a keen (albeit somewhat incomplete) sense of honor, he cringed before no man and obeyed only the commands of his own conscience. Second, he was brave: strong in muscle and nerve, able to endure hardship, and too proud ever to flee from danger. Even Dr. Ravenel, who calls Southerners "barbarians," admits that they are a testimony to the fortitude of the human race. Third, the Southern gentleman was exquisitely well-mannered, was, indeed, "a school of politeness" that spread social grace wherever he went. Miss Ravenel says that the "better classes" of the South are charming at dinner parties, generous, and courteous, and she considers such demeanor the hallmark of civilization. The chivalrous Southron thus combined the dignity and savoir-faire of a French aristocrat with the simple courage of a Pequot warrior. The high-toned gentleman epitomized the best qualities of the past, and De Forest hoped those qualities might be "engrafted" onto the present.[3]

On the other hand, De Forest made it clear that he was glad to see the chivalrous Southron go. The consistent message of De Forest's writings in the 1860s was that the way of life that produced the chivalrous Southron also produced intolerable evils: the systematic violation of human liberty and the demoralization of the Southern people. De Forest summarized both his praise and his condemnation of the South when he described the high-toned gentleman as one "who scorned work, loved authority, preferred death to shame, fought heroically for his own rights and ignored those of others." To bring about a truly honorable society, the Southern way of life had to be destroyed, and along with it would go the chivalrous Southron. That type, De Forest said, "cannot be preserved, much less re-created, in a democracy of labor." Like the Indians of Connecticut, the gentlemen of the Confederacy were standing in the way of progress.[4]

Most particularly, most basically, most egregiously, Southrons were standing in the way of human equality, an objective De Forest had only recently come to honor. Reared in a family that aspired to gentility, he could not help complaining about having his social inferiors—"tinkers" and "boors"—as his brother officers. At the same time, however, he conceived of the Civil War as an attempt to abolish such social discrimination. As Dr. Ravenel says, it is a "democratic struggle which confirms the masses in an equality with the few." De Forest viewed the South as the land of radical inequality, with plantation aristocrats domineering slaves and lower-class whites alike. By the cruel artifices of law and custom, the Southern people were divided into castes with different rights, opportunities, expectations, and obligations. In contrast, De Forest saw the North as the land of equality, with all people treated the same. He did not doubt that the North was on the side of the angels. During the Civil War, Jacksonian democracy finally caught up with J. W. De Forest.[5]

In *Miss Ravenel's Conversion,* the lawyer-turned-soldier Edward Colburne is described as a "representative of a staid puritanical aristocracy," but as a captain in the Union army he proves himself a democrat. The men in his company are common folk—farmers and masons, swamp Yankees and Irishmen—but he is proud of them. Though they are as weak and self-indulgent as other New Englanders at the start of the war, they undergo the hardships of forced marches, sieges, and attacks; develop stamina and discipline; and become as fearsome as bulldogs. Colburne warms into grandiloquence when he writes of his men: "Oh, these noblemen of nature, our American common soldiers! In the face of suffering and death they are my equals; and while I exact their obedience, I accord them my respect." When Colburne mentions officers who come from the lower classes in civilian life, he says that they represent the "plain people whose cause is being fought out in this war against aristocracy." Captain Colburne, like Captain De Forest, is glad to fight for their cause.[6]

Colburne respects his men for being good soldiers, and they, in a sort of democratic reciprocity, judge him in exactly the same way. They do not honor him for his high social class. Indeed, they make a joke of his genteel background and aspirations. They are impressed, though, when they find that he can march as far and as fast as anyone else in the company—and without complaining. In the army, says Colburne, "distinctions are rubbed out; it is who can fight best, march best, command best; each one stands on the base of his individual manhood." Not even rank can compel respect as competence can. The men despise Major Gazaway, who is laid low by "sickness" before every battle; but they admire Captain Colburne, who has the courage to fight. The soldiers thus judge each other according to criteria that men of all classes, whether "puritanical aristocracy" or "plain people," can meet.[7]

De Forest's own critique of aristocracy is made obvious by his handling of a minor character in the novel named Lieutenant Van Zandt. The lieutenant, who serves as an aide to Captain Colburne, is a member of one of the fine old families of New York, and he never for a moment forgets that he comes from "Knickerbocker" stock. He honors a man who is born and bred a gentleman rather than "one of those plebeian humbugs whom our ridiculous Democracy delights to call nature's gentlemen." Yet, although Van Zandt is a mouthpiece for the aristocracy, he is not a mouthpiece for De Forest. The lieutenant is a drunkard, a ne'er-do-well, a braggart, a fool—in short, as Colburne says, "a reprobate." His very existence refutes the idea of class superiority. By portraying the depravity of the born gentleman, De Forest locates himself on the side of "our ridiculous Democracy."[8]

De Forest's new-found egalitarianism was put to the test when he examined a group in whom he had never found much to admire: the "low-down people" (Greenville's name for poor whites). The "cracker," De Forest said, was quarrelsome and lawless, lazy and unproductive, and his "only service to society was to drive off the still more worthless Indian." De Forest remained enough of an aristocrat to make no secret of his disdain for the poor. It is important to note, however, De Forest's explanation of the *cause* of the low-down people's debasement. It was caused, he said, not by some inherent defect in members of the class but by the social and economic system into which they had been born—by nurture rather than by nature. Living in a culture that devalued self-respect and self-reliance, the poor had little opportunity to acquire those qualities. Still, it was not impossible to do so. Some "now respectable" Southern families had started out as low-downers. "Their birth was a barrier to their success," said De Forest, "but not an impassable one." If the social system were changed so as to encourage independence, then even more low-downers might rise. Although De Forest had little fondness for poor whites, he believed that individuals of that class, as among all other classes, had the potential to be "respectable." In that sense, the low-downers were equal to the aristocrats.[9]

Any discussion of equality in the 1860s led almost inevitably to the question of race, and in this matter De Forest shared the views of many whites living somewhere north of slavery. Before the Civil War, he disparaged the "ragged, . . . drunken or rowdy" free blacks of New Haven's "Coontown." While serving in the Union army, he referred to his black orderlies as a "fat and dirty nigger," a "blubber-lipped loafer," and a "little yellow vagrant." After North and South had been reunited, he convincingly denied "the supposed love of the Yankee for the nigger." De Forest, clearly, was not without prejudice. It is also clear, however, that De Forest's racism was counterbalanced, during the years he spent in uniform, by a belief in equality. Although he never overcame his sense of racial superiority, he now was sufficiently egalitarian to call it into question. He was now able to doubt his own beliefs.[10]

This was apparent, for example, when he considered the problem of intelligence. On the one hand, he emphatically declared that "the Negro as he is, no matter how educated, is not the mental equal of the European." De Forest began his article on "The Man and Brother" by telling a story about a freedman that showed "how ignorant and simple and childish he can be." On the other hand, De Forest drew a distinction between *can be* and *is*. Although the black man could be ignorant as a child, he could also be like Cato Allums, the freedman who successfully defended himself against assault and whom De Forest described as "a fine, stalwart, vigorous fellow"—and a clever horse trader. Observing Reconstruction in South Carolina, De Forest reported that blacks had testified honestly in court, voted responsibly in elections, and taken pains to secure education for their children—hardly signs of stupidity. Moreover, even when asserting that blacks were intellectually inferior to whites, De Forest attributed that inferiority not to insurmountable biology but to cultural factors that could, in time, be changed. He argued that being raised as slaves had deprived blacks of the opportunity to develop their minds: "they lacked the forcing influence of highly educated competition and of a refined home influence." Saying that a man's chances "go very far" toward making him what he is, De Forest suggested that blacks, once freed and once provided with intellectual challenge and domestic advantages, could improve their minds. As Dr. Ravenel puts it, "You will find them bright enough if you won't knock them on the head."[11]

De Forest thought that the long history of enslavement, extended not merely for one lifetime but for generations, had prevented blacks from keeping up with the intellectual progress of whites. Living in freedom had "forced" white individuals to become more intelligent, De Forest believed, and their higher intelligence had then been passed along to their offspring: characteristics acquired in one generation had been inherited by the next. Blacks, in contrast, had lacked the stimulus of freedom and therefore had developed little mental improvement to pass on to their children. As a result, De Forest argued, free whites had become brighter at a faster rate than enslaved blacks: "ancestral intelligence, trained through generations of study, must tell, even though the rival thinking machines may be naturally of the same calibre." In this way, De Forest explained what he perceived as an important intellectual difference between the white and black races.[12]

This belief in the inheritance of ancestral intelligence supported racism and subverted it at the same time. It supported racism by asserting that blacks were presently less intelligent than whites and that only with the slow passing of generations could blacks attain the intellectual level of whites. Conversely, the belief undermined racism by affirming both the possibility that blacks originally had "thinking machines" equal to those of whites and also the possibility that blacks eventually could once again achieve an equal "calibre." The great planter, the low-downer, and the freedman all shared the same human nature. It was this essential sameness that justified equal rights for all races and emancipation. For De Forest, as for Dr. Ravenel, the Civil War was "a struggle for the freedom of all men, without distinction of race or color."[13]

One indication of the weakened condition of De Forest's racism during the 1860s was the ambivalence with which he discussed the Anglo-Saxon "race." After saying that blacks and Chinese were peaceable folk who rarely got into fights, he drew an interesting comparison with his own people: "Anglo-Saxons are the most belligerent race, either as individuals or as peoples, that the world now contains; and yet they have been of far greater service in advancing the interests of humanity than Negroes or Chinamen; at least they will tell you so, and whip you into admitting it." As the second independent clause of the sentence indicates, De Forest suspected that Anglo-Saxons, despite their belligerence, were superior to other races; as the third clause indicates, however, he had some doubt about it. When describing in another article the debauchery of low-downers, he noted that these dissolute people were one variety of "our much boasted Anglo-Saxon race." Such jabs directed at racist ideas demonstrated his susceptibility to egalitarian ones.[14]

Thus, although De Forest could not entirely leave behind his patrician contempt for plebeians, especially if they were black, he had evolved into something of an ideological democrat. Denying that nature had divided humankind into races and classes with immutable and fundamentally different moral and intellectual qualities, he said that people must be judged as individuals, not as members of a race or a class. Every tub had to stand on its own bottom. This kind of democratic individualism, he believed, was prevalent in the North but not in the South. In the North, a man from the lower ranks of society could earn recognition as a "nobleman of nature"; not so in the South, where the common white man—not to mention the black slave—was inevitably despised. The failure to appreciate the equality of mankind and the failure to reward the achievement of individuals marked the South, in De Forest's eyes, as a primitive society. When, in *Miss Ravenel's Conversion,* he contrasted the "barbarian" South to the "truly free and democratic North," he left no doubt in the reader's mind that Northern society was more just and that the Southern way of life, however charming it might sometimes be, deserved the extinction to which the Union army was consigning it.[15]

De Forest believed that the South's undemocratic civilization, aside from being intrinsically unjust, also produced a host of evil consequences. To begin with, it undermined the pride of most Southerners. De Forest admired the chivalrous Southron's self-respect, and he urged other Americans to copy it; however, he deplored the South for developing that self-respect only in the upper class. De Forest believed that the South honored only gentlemen, not yeomen or working men, and that such discrimination annihilated the dignity of the masses, both black and white. He compared the "feudal, somewhat patriarchal" system of the South to that of a race of monkeys who desperately cling to their "central monkey" (the high-toned gentleman) and always follow his lead. Such servility disgusted the apostle of individualism. Saying that the "cracker" was always subservient, first to the planters and then to the Yankee conquerors, De Forest despised him for possessing "no self-respect and no moral courage." Remembering the revulsion he had felt a decade earlier for the beggars on the island of Rhodes, he said that the Southern poor white "revered power like an Oriental and put his mouth in the dust before whomsoever represented it." De Forest thus believed that Southern civilization produced self-respect only in a small minority while reducing the vast majority to submissiveness. He much preferred Northern democracy, which, he believed, awarded esteem to individuals of all classes and thereby produced a nation of proud and dignified men.[16]

Democracy, De Forest thought, produced not only self-respect but also another element of individualism, namely, self-reliance. In a democratic society where every man stood on his own legs, everyone found it necessary to work. If he were to prosper or even to survive, he had to provide for himself. In an aristocratic society, however, some men lived off the labor of others; in the South, the slave toiled while his master relaxed in perpetual dissipation. The democratic system encouraged labor by associating it with upward mobility. The aristocratic system discouraged labor by associating it with slavery. In the South, De Forest believed, work was despised by whites and blacks alike. To blacks it meant drudgery without hope of reward; to whites it meant being black. Like many other observers, De Forest saw quite a difference between the industrious North and the lazy South, a difference that seemed to prove the superior virtue of the North. Like Dr. Ravenel, De Forest believed that "the great elementary duty of man" was "working for his own subsistence." As a Union officer in the Reconstruction, De Forest intended to teach Southerners their duty.[17]

In his capacity as agent for the Freedmen's Bureau, De Forest led the federal war on poverty in his district. The Civil War had ruined the farms and businesses of many people around Greenville, had made widows and orphans of others, and had left many more unemployed. De Forest's strategy during the hard winter of 1866–1867, however, was not to dispense relief but to withhold it. At both the national and state levels, leaders of the bureau were trying to minimize relief to avoid waste and to promote self-reliance; however, De Forest's zeal for economy exceeded even that of his superiors. Believing that "what a man does not work for is of no permanent value to him," he refused to distribute even the limited supply of food and clothing the bureau had made available. He did so, he explained, to root out laziness.

> If I had drawn rations for thirty old Negroes whose decrepitude could not be questioned, three hundred other old Negroes, whose claims were almost equally good, would have presented themselves. The watchword of "draw day" would have spread like a fiery cross over two thousand square miles of country, bringing into Greenville many hundreds of people who otherwise might remain at work. . . . The fact that my poor were chiefly low-down whites who needed to be spurred to work, or venerable Negroes who were tolerably well cared for by charitable planters, enabled me long to resist that humane impulse which detests general laws and calls for special providences.[18]

Occasionally, however, special providences were unavoidable. In March 1867, Congress authorized a distribution of corn and bacon to the Southern poor, and even De Forest acknowledged that the distress was so acute as to require relief. Rather than hand out rations to all comers, however, De Forest set up a system that aimed at assuring the food got to the people—white as well as black—who needed it most. After obtaining lists of destitute persons from forty local magistrates, he entrusted those magistrates with dispensing the goods to the people on those lists. Insofar as the officials carried out their duties fairly and thoroughly, the relief program was efficient. Nonetheless, De Forest was unhappy with it. He stopped the dole as soon as he could, he returned surplus grain to the government, and he said in retrospect that the distribution did as much harm as good: "It alleviated a considerable amount of suffering, prevented possibly a few cases of starvation, seduced many thousands of people from work, and fostered a spirit of idleness and beggary."[19]

For a man who had spent most of his adult life living off his relatives' earnings, De Forest made much of self-reliance. So chary was he of encouraging indolence that he actively discouraged generosity. Finding the freedmen "extravagant in giving," he lamented that the successful farmers gave away their surplus produce to poor relations rather than convert it into capital. White Southerners, too, showed this demoralizing benevolence, feeding every beggar who came to the door and setting bounteous tables for regular and ravenous guests. "People who lived on

Negroes," observed the Yankee with regret, "felt it right to live on each other and to help each other." Among both races he found that "the industrious were too much given to supporting the thriftless."[20]

De Forest viewed this excessive charity as a symptom of the South's backwardness in social organization. He had seen similar "thoughtless generosity," he said, among the Syrians "and other semi-civilized races." They, too, had received "an imperfect moral education as to the distinction between *meum* and *tuum*" and had not learned that every man has a "full right" to his property. Southerners' generosity "was not that Yankee generosity which sends pundits to convert Hottentots, founds school systems, hospitals, sanitary commissions, and endows colleges with millions. It was the old-fashioned sort, the generosity of the Arab and of the feudal noble." Whereas modern Yankee philanthropy stimulated improvement, the antiquated Southern variety deadened all desire for progress. Whereas Yankee gifts were investments that yielded perpetual returns, Southern gifts were splurges that left no capital behind. If "reconstruction" were to have any meaning for De Forest, it would provide Southerners with the proper "moral education" regarding work and property.[21]

In his writings of the 1860s, De Forest repeatedly portrayed the American South as a primitive civilization that had somehow persisted into modern times but that now had to be destroyed. The "slaveholding Sodom," as Dr. Ravenel describes it, "must be razed and got out of the way, like any other obstacle to the progress of humanity. It must make room for something more consonant with the railroad, electric-telegraph, printing-press, inductive philosophy, and practical Christianity." However interesting the anachronism might be, and whatever charm it might possess, the South could not be allowed to keep up "the social systems of the middle ages." When Dr. Ravenel sees "the progress of our race from barbarism to civilization" and when Captain Colburne insists (like Galileo) that "the world does move," both of them prophesy the extinction of the Southern way of life. They also describe the plot of *Miss Ravenel's Conversion*.[22]

It is unfortunate that Lillie Ravenel is among the less memorable characters in the remarkable novel that bears her name. Pretty, pure, and not excessively bright, she is doomed eventually to marry the equally tedious Edward Colburne. The discriminating reader's attention inevitably veers away from Miss Ravenel and toward more interesting personages: Madame Larue and Colonel Carter, or even Dr. Ravenel and Lieutenant Van Zandt. Because of Miss Ravenel's insipidness, it is easy to overlook her importance, to ignore the fact that the entire story hinges on her "conversion." But if one wishes to discover the thought of J. W. De Forest, one must attend to Miss Ravenel. Her biography is the novel's philosophy.

Lillie enters the novel as a barbarian. Like Harriet De Forest, she has lived in the South and has liked it. Seeing nothing wrong with the undemocratic society there, she hopes for a Confederate victory in the war. Even after Northern troops conquer Louisiana and the Ravenels return to the South, she wants her father to become a planter, a "sugar aristocrat," and she believes that his role in Reconstruction should be to restore runaway slaves to their rightful owners. Naturally, she quarrels with the abolitionist Colburne. The surest demonstration of Miss Ravenel's "barbarian beliefs" occurs when she drops Colburne and marries Colonel John Carter, a Virginia aristocrat who, although loyal to the Union, would probably own slaves if he had not squandered his family fortune. Lillie herself is hardly parsimonious. Delighted when her husband buys her a carriage and a pair of ponies, she reinforces his habit of living beyond his means. She shares the fiscal recklessness of the Southerners she adores.[23]

Carter epitomizes the chivalrous Southron. He is a self-assured man of the world who looks women straight in the eye and who makes a shy Yankee like Colburne seem to "shrink to grasshopper mediocrity." Carter is a man of broad shoulders and bristling moustache, a man whose courage has been proven on the field of battle, a man's man. He also, however, is a ladies' man, a bon vivant who conducts himself in the drawing room with witty audacity and unerring delicacy. He is, in short, "a true child of his class and State," and he proves more than a match for Colburne in competing for the hand of Miss Ravenel. Colonel Carter is "this 'high-toned' gentleman whom she insists upon having." Unfortunately for Miss Ravenel, however, the colonel turns out to be more high-toned than high-minded. After his spendthrift habits get him heavily into debt, he defrauds the government of thousands of dollars. After marrying Miss Ravenel, he has an affair with the delectable Madame Larue (another well-born Southerner). Carter thus represents not only the charm of the South but also its unkindness. First glances can be deceiving.[24]

Meanwhile, even before Lillie has learned of her husband's misbehavior, she has already begun her conversion. She finds the South not quite the delightful country she had remembered. Because her father sides with the Yankees, she too is insulted and ostracized by spiteful secessionists. Southern hospitality, indeed, is strikingly absent. One evening when Dr. Ravenel goes walking, he is clubbed to the ground by a rebel—an event that starts Miss Ravenel on the road to conversion. "The moment a Southern ruffian knocked her father on the head, she began to see that Secession was indefensible, and that the American Union ought to be preserved."[25]

The next step in the conversion process occurs when Lillie discovers the affair between her husband and Madame Larue. After a painful awakening, Lillie leaves Carter, leaves the South with all its traitors and betrayers, and heads for the more decent society of the North. Meanwhile, her husband, who is campaigning in the field, meets his death at the Battle of Cane River. This event leaves Lillie free to marry again, and this time she chooses Captain Colburne, "the man whom she ought always to have loved." By now, however, Colburne is a changed man, much different from the awkward, diffident young lawyer he was when Miss Ravenel first rejected him for Colonel Carter. Having served in combat as a captain of volunteers, Colburne has developed physical hardihood and the habit of command. Having been stationed for a time in the refined purlieus of New Orleans, he has learned to speak French, to drink cognac (in moderate quantities), and to banter pleasingly with ladies. The Yankee now is everything Miss Ravenel could want. With her new husband and her new understanding of men and politics, Lillie no longer hankers after Southerners and the South. When Colburne asks her if she would ever again like to live in New Orleans, she gives an answer that shows how completely she has changed. "Oh, never!" she replies. "Always at the North! I like it so much better!" Lillie has even conquered her barbaric habit of thriftlessness. After becoming engaged to Colburne and beginning to furnish their future home, she plans not to entertain much for a while because she knows they cannot yet afford it. Indeed, she has become so frugal that she postpones their honeymoon until five years after their wedding. She has become a genuine Yankee. Her conversion is complete.[26]

When the Union defeats the Confederacy and when Colburne supplants Carter as the husband of Lillie Ravenel, both processes seem as inevitable as the passage of time. The chivalrous Southron is an anachronism, a barbarian in a civilized era, an aristocrat in an age of democracy. He is as brave and proud as an Indian warrior; he also is equally perfidious, destructive, and doomed. The chapter in which Lillie goes back to the North and Carter goes to his death is entitled "A Most Logical Conclusion." The full name of the novel, *Miss Ravenel's Conversion from Secession to Loyalty,* echoes John Bunyan's *The Pilgrim's Progress from This World to That Which Is to Come,* and both books tell of a journey from a City of Destruction to a Celestial City. While the Pilgrim progresses from this world of sin to that of glory that is to come, Miss Ravenel progresses from the aristocratic world that we have lost to this democratic one of today. Miss Ravenel's conversion is the repudiation of the past, the embracing of the present, the conquest of nostalgia.[27]

As long as the Civil War and Reconstruction lasted, J. W. De Forest was a happy man. After years of being an invalid, he was proving himself rugged. After living like a parasite on the body of his hard-working and prosperous relatives, he finally was earning a steady income of his own. After the alienation of being a gentleman in a Jacksonian world, he was joining the "plain people" in their fight for equality. After bemoaning the lack of great men in post-Revolutionary America, he was rejoicing at the emergence of Lincoln and Grant and a million blue-coated "noblemen of nature." Everywhere De Forest looked, he saw moral and material improvement.

In the mid-1860s, De Forest wrote with a distinctly optimistic tone. Confident that his country was in the hands of brave and decent men, he could speak of it with pride and affection. Secure in the knowledge that scoundrels and brutes had been defeated, he could afford to describe even *them* with sympathy. He could examine the human condition with more delight than disgust, more admiration than scorn. Occasionally, of course, he would show revulsion, as when he observed the low-downers of Greenville. For the most part, however, he wrote in a spirit of curiosity and good will. It was in this frame of mind that he produced his finest works.

In making a parable of the passing of the old order, for example, he achieved a high order of comedy:

> It was indescribably amusing to watch a Charlestonian friend of mine during his first and last visit to New York. Dressed in a full suit of black, and bearing a gold-headed cane in his hand, he walked Broadway at the dignified rate of two and a half miles an hour. Some one brushed against his right elbow: he turned and glared, grasping his cane tightly; the intruder was gone. Some one brushed against his left elbow; another pause, glare, and settling of the cane in the fist: no antagonist visible. Every few steps he felt himself insulted, he prepared to vindicate his honor, and he failed to discover any one whom he could call to account. At the end of six blocks, fuming with a consciousness of aggravated injuries, he took a carriage, drove back to the St. Nicholas, drank a mint julep, seated himself in a window of the reading room, and stared sullenly at the interminable crowd which hurried by unaware of his existence. He was like a cat who should be hustled and intimidated by a garret-full of scrabbling mice. Within a week he left the city thoroughly disgusted with its multitudinous bustle, and never returned to it.[28]

This description of a chivalrous Southron crushed by "the friction of a hurried democracy" evinces not only compassion for the victim but also affection for his energetic assailants. The passage condemns no one, complains of nothing. De Forest is in such good humor that he merely observes and enjoys.

So he did also when he portrayed Colonel Carter and Madame Larue. Carter and Larue are adulterers, liars, swindlers; they also are wonderfully likable. De Forest does not excuse the miscreants, but he describes them with a relish that might almost be mistaken for approval. When Carter fights his last battle, he does not seem like a bad man about to receive his just deserts, but like a brave man doing his job:

> He was on horseback closely following his advancing brigade and watching its spirited push and listening to its mad yell with such a smile of soldierly delight and pride that it was a pleasure to look upon his bronzed, confident, heroic face. It would have been strange to a civilian to hear the stream of joyful curses with which he expressed his admiration and elation.
> "God damn them! see them go in!" he said. "God damn their souls! I can put them anywhere!"

After Carter is struck by a bullet, a chaplain tries to save the colonel's soul by imploring him to think of the sacrifice of Jesus Christ. Carter, however, is a good soldier who keeps his mind on one world at a time. "Don't bother!" he tells the chaplain. "Where is the brigade?" At a moment like this, it is hard for the reader not to admire the sinner more than the saint.[29]

Nor can one despise Madame Larue, the other great invention of the novel. It is not merely the widow's dark eyes, her plump arms, her deep bosom, or her invitingly liberal morals that make her irresistible to the reader; it is also her cleverness. Her racy conversation makes Lillie Ravenel seem dimwitted by comparison, and her adroit manipulation of others is a cause of astonishment. One of the most fascinating scenes in the novel occurs after Colburne, single-mindedly devoted to Miss Ravenel, rejects an amorous offer from Madame Larue. The scorned woman obtains a beautiful revenge by asking Colburne, with Lillie present, about his attendance at banquets sponsored by light-skinned Negroes of New Orleans. Inquiring whether he prefers white people or brown, Madame Larue forces him to defend the loyalty, breeding, and appearance of the octoroons—thus offending the ferociously Anglo-Saxon Miss Ravenel. When Colburne begins to lose his temper, Madame Larue apologizes for upsetting him and meekly explains that she had not meant to scold him but only to let him know, in a gentle way, that people of mixed blood are not received in the polite society of New Orleans. Her eyes seem so full of penitence that Colburne feels as if he has wronged her. The result of it all is that Miss Ravenel is "detached" from Colburne, Colburne feels ashamed for abusing an innocent lady, and the reader cannot help admiring the ruthless genius of Madame Larue. Like Colonel Carter, she extorts her share of respect.[30]

Nothing better illustrates De Forest's good-natured tolerance than his discussion of alcohol. As a boy, De Forest took the pledge of abstinence; in his later writings, he frequently sermonized on the evils of drink; and *Miss Ravenel's Conversion* contains one such diatribe. Nevertheless, the rest of the book presents drinking, even drunkenness, as a spectacle causing amusement rather than indignation. Lieutenant Van Zandt's bibulous denunciation of Major Gazaway as "a damn incur-dam-able dam coward" and Carter's awakening into the wooly and feverish world of a hangover are pleasing scenes. One of the funnier lines of the book occurs after Carter has delivered a disquisition on man's ability to stave off drunkenness through the application of will power. He says that the only time he completely lost his self-control was when he was obligated to spend a night in "the dolefullest, cursedest place" on earth, namely, Cairo, Illinois. "If a man is excusable anywhere for drinking himself insensible," explains the colonel, "it is at Cairo, Illinois." The temperance man De Forest thus finds himself in sympathy with a man on a binge. The novelist could hardly be more liberal than that.[31]

De Forest's most famous essay in literary criticism, "The Great American Novel," possesses the same confident tone and optimistic point of view. Although De Forest complains of the American people's failure to buy the works of native authors, his main point is that writers have not done justice to the American people by producing a great novel that accurately portrays the "ordinary emotions and manners of American existence." James Fenimore Cooper, for example, created idealized characters who were "less natural than the wax figures of Barnum's old museum." Oliver Wendell Holmes wrote defter prose but restricted his view to New England, thus producing stories that were merely provincial, not truly "American." Nathaniel Hawthorne looked deep into men's hearts, but his characters "are what Yankees might come to be who should shut themselves up for life to meditate in old manses. They have no sympathy with this eager and laborious people, which takes so many newspapers, builds so many railroads, does the most business on a given capital, wages the biggest war in proportion to its population, believes in the physically impossible and does some of it." De Forest had so much affection for this "eager and laborious people" that he soared into hyperbole when describing them, and he criticized other novelists for failing to depict them completely and exactly.[32]

He himself had recently made the attempt to depict America in *Miss Ravenel's Conversion.* That novel includes Americans from many regions and many walks of life, and it portrays those characters with uncommon truthfulness. In its characterizations as well as its patriotic theme, it is a celebration of the American people—a tribute to the author's time and place. De Forest's exuberant description of Americans was one more testament to his happy state of mind, a state that would last as long as he was a soldier.

Near the end of the nineteenth century, when De Forest looked back over his long career, he said that *Miss Ravenel's Conversion* was the earliest of his novels with which he was satisfied. *Witching Times* and *Seacliff* had been "very poor things," but in *Miss Ravenel's Conversion,* "for the first time in my life I came to know the value of personal knowledge of one's subject and the art of drawing upon life for one's characters." Although in 1867 De Forest did not yet use the word *realism,* it was realism that, more than anything else, made *Miss Ravenel's Conversion* noteworthy, and it was that noteworthy novel that established the benchmark of De Forest's fiction.[33]

The book's realism consisted of the scrupulous re-invention of the actual world rather than the fabrication of a new world from materials unknown to human experience. Because De Forest had learned "the art of drawing upon life for one's characters," the people in *Miss Ravenel's Conversion* are the sort one might actually meet at a picnic in New Haven. Colburne may be irksomely upright, and Lillie may bubble with more innocence than anyone ought to have, but some people are like that (or at least they used to be, in New Haven). Madame Larue and Colonel Carter lead lives that are shameful, criminal, but not at all incredible. When *Harper's* reviewed De Forest's novel, the critic noted the "total freedom from exaggeration in the portraiture" and approved the way in which "a man or a woman may be weak or wrong in some ways without being wholly devilish." William Dean Howells, who was just discovering "Mr. De Forrest," said that the people in *Miss Ravenel's Conversion* were "so unlike characters in novels as to be like people in life"—and that was just what the author intended.[34]

Then, too, the situations in the novel—the settings and the turns of the plot—were plausible. Because De Forest knew "the value of personal knowledge of one's subjects," he placed his characters in circumstances he himself had witnessed and that the reader knew to exist. Whether making small talk at the supper table or ducking bullets during a siege, De Forest's characters live in a universe not much different from the reader's own. The achievement of the realist, something of a miracle, is to create fiction out of fact.

Miss Ravenel's Conversion contained much of the strongest writing De Forest would ever do; it also, however, contained some very feeble passages that foreshadowed one of the disasters of his later fiction. De Forest was at his best when he appealed to the reader's intellect by illuminating the inconspicuous events, the "tittle-tattle" of everyday life. He was at his worst when he tried to excite the emotions by depicting tremendous joy or sorrow. Probably the worst scene in *Miss Ravenel's Conversion* occurs when Colburne's mother is dying:

> A few broken words, a murmuring of unutterable, unearthly, infinite happiness, echoes as it were of greetings far away with welcoming angels, were her last utterances. To the young man, who still held her hand and now and then kissed

her cheek, she seemed to slumber, although her breathing gradually sank so low that he could not perceive it. But after a long time the nurse came to the bedside, bent over it, looked, listened, and said, "She is gone!"[35]

Fortunately the book makes few such sallies into the land of high emotions.

This restraint is remarkable in a war story. Considering the opportunities combat scenes offer, it is surprising how little passion the book attempts to portray. Cowards are depicted, but fear is not. (As De Forest later said, "I actually did not dare state the extreme horror of battle, and the anguish with which the bravest soldiers struggle through it."[36]) When Colonel Carter is mortally wounded, he does not attend to present or future torment, he thinks about winning the battle. His death scene, deprived of sentiment, is much better written than that of Colburne's mother. The Civil War produced many occasions of passion, but De Forest left them for romantics like Stephen Crane. His own gift lay along other lines. Unfortunately, he would sometimes forget that fact.

Chapter 6

His business does not keep him, and so he works carelessly at it, or he quits it.

J. W. De Forest, "The Great American Novel," 1868

When, in 1868, J. W. De Forest committed himself to full-time writing, he found himself in a dilemma. To obtain the leisure required for attempting a great novel, he had to give up his post in the Freedmen's Bureau. His resignation, however, left him without a steady salary and compelled him to make a living with his pen. To do so, he had to produce works that would appeal to a large but obtuse audience whose attitude toward genuine literature ranged from indifference to positive hostility. Writing for such a public, De Forest did not have greatness forced upon him. Between 1868 and 1881, he turned out dozens of short stories and articles, two novellas, and at least eight novels[1]—none of which equalled *Miss Ravenel's Conversion* as an artistic achievement. When De Forest ceased being an amateur writer and became a professional, he ceased producing his finest work.

The decade of the 1870s witnessed a decline not only in De Forest's literary accomplishment but also in his personal life. After resigning his commission in the army, he fretted more than ever about how to make ends meet. Moreover, he lost the conviction that he was doing something useful. Now, as during the 1850s, his conscience nagged him for being a mere scribbler rather than a man of action. Also, as the years went by, he grew ever more solitary. His wife died, his son left home, and De Forest was left entirely to himself. One thing that did *not* change after 1868 was his health; it remained bad. Neuralgia and dyspepsia aggravated his accumulated injuries of heart and mind.

In the article in which De Forest revealed his desire to produce a great American novel, he also acknowledged that producing it would not be easy. Because there was no international copyright law, he said, the American market was flooded by cheap, pirated editions of books by foreign authors. As a result, the American writer earned little for his labor—a demoralizing circumstance that prevented him from contributing to a distinctive and distinguished American literature. "His business does not keep him," reported De Forest, "and so he works carelessly at it, or he quits it."[2] Having once (in 1859) given up novel writing to pursue the more remunerative occupations of journalism and soldiery, De Forest spoke from experience. Even though he returned to fiction, he had not forgotten the importance of revenue. To make his work salable, he chose subjects he thought would please a large audience, no matter how little he knew or cared about such subjects. He did not deliberately write badly. He did, however, deliberately select plots and settings that made it difficult for him to write well.

In 1869, while trying to place the story "The Oversoul of Manse Roseburgh" with the *Galaxy* magazine, De Forest explained to the editors the philosophy behind his latest composition. Saying that "the tale of ordinary life no longer excites remark, no matter how well done" and that "the day for easy success of commonplace subjects & good writing is over," he described his new strategy. "What I try to do," he said, "is to sketch realistic characters & put them through a series of extraordinary and even grotesque circumstances." Such sensationalism was an obvious change in an author who had previously boasted that his forte was tittle-tattle, and the reason for the change was equally obvious. Stories of the extraordinary and grotesque, he said, would be "pretty sure to make talk, & that brings readers."[3]

When he attempted to put realistic characters into grotesque circumstances, however, the characters became as absurd as their circumstances. In "The Oversoul of Manse Roseburgh," for example, the love of young Susie Ridley transformed the rakish and debauched Mansfield Roseburgh into the very model of propriety. "As the sun draws leaves and flowers from the bare stalks of spring," wrote De Forest in a typical passage, "so her affection had drawn profuse and sweet sentiment from his hitherto sterile soul." The transformation of personality was so "extraordinary" as to be implausible, and De Forest knew it. "Someday," he wrote,

> Roseburgh will more or less go back from this noble largeness of expression, to his old and own personality. That day he may, or he may not, become a bad husband, first unsympathetic, then faithless, then loveless, then cruel.
> But if ardent, persistent, self-sacrificing affection can keep him in the right and happy way, he will be kept there by his wife.

De Forest, who not long before had created the incorrigible roué Colonel John Carter, knew that leopards did not change their spots, but now he pretended not to know.[4]

There was only one thing that prevented "The Oversoul of Manse Roseburgh" from being a total failure: it paid. To De Forest's surprise, the *Galaxy* did not merely accept the story but also sent him $150—more than his usual price. This act of generosity must have strengthened De Forest's determination to ignore everyday reality and to write instead about the unlikely. It may also have led him to produce the novel *Overland,* which the *Galaxy* published as a serial from August 1870 to July 1871 and which was issued as a volume in the latter year.[5]

Overland shows how badly a good novelist can write. A tale that meanders from Sante Fe to the Pacific, it consists of a series of hairbreadth escapes from Indian attacks, murder by poison and bullet, starvation, thirst, sickness, and accidental drowning in river and sea. Much of the book is given over to unconvincing descriptions of geological formations, Indians, Wild West artifacts, and other curiosities about which De Forest had read in the Yale College library. The characters—the "tall, full-chested, finely-limbed" Lieutenant Ralph Thurstane, the modest maiden Clara Van Diemen, the treacherous Mexican Carlos Coronado, and a horde of brutal Apaches—might be considered wooden, had they possessed a little more natural suppleness and vitality. The author himself confesses that the tale provides "little more than a superficial view of the characters of our people. Events, incidents, adventures, and even landscapes have been the leading personages of the story." The book possesses in abundance the extraordinary and grotesque circumstances that were intended to make talk and bring readers.[6]

Yet, it has its good moments. During a storm at sea, "from two of the staterooms came sounds which plainly confessed that the occupants were having a bad night of it"; or when a flatterer addresses a fool, "'You are the greatest woman of our times,' he said, stepping backward a pace or two and surveying her as if she were a cathedral."[7] When De Forest can forsake great adventures and can attend instead to the fine details of ordinary life, his prose becomes original. Unfortunately, such moments come rarely in this book.

Overland was a success of the same order as "The Oversoul of Manse Roseburgh." According to a later newspaper account, it was one of De Forest's most popular books. A teenager named Brander Matthews read it eagerly as it appeared month by month in the *Galaxy*; and later, when he was a noted drama critic and scholar, he remembered it as a "rattling good yarn." (When De Forest planned a second edition of the book, he intended to add a subtitle: "A Story for Boys.") Along with popularity came profitability. De Forest received one hundred dollars for each of the twelve installments in the *Galaxy*, plus 10 percent from the sale of the volume, thus making *Overland* a far more valuable piece of merchandise than *Miss Ravenel's Conversion*.[8]

Not even *Overland*, however, was enough to make De Forest into a celebrity. In a letter to William Dean Howells in 1871, De Forest said he was discouraged by a newspaper story about American novels that reported "that De Forest is doing good work 'almost unnoticed,'" and he wondered how he could generate more notice. He placed hope in a vigorous advertising campaign for *Overland* when it appeared as a volume; "trumpeting," he said, was as potent in America as it had been around Jericho. He also, however, hoped to spread his fame by publishing the kind of fiction the public seemed to crave. He told Howells, editor of the prestigious but narrowly circulating *Atlantic,* that the magazine appealed too much to "Mr. Emerson & other select Bostonians" and not enough to the "great herd of young people, eager to browse upon romance." Stressing the need for large doses of "sentiment," he offered to inject additional "stimulus" into his own novel, *Kate Beaumont,* which was currently appearing in the magazine.[9]

The novel had sentiment aplenty. Situated in antebellum South Carolina and focusing on a family feud between the tidewater Beaumonts and the upcountry McAlisters, it tells of the troubled courtship of Kate Beaumont and Frank McAlister. After their two families wear each other down with insults, duels, and actual murder, the star-crossed lovers are finally united. When Frank proposes marriage to Kate, he

> sought her amid a perfumed tangle of shrubbery and flowers. The faint golden radiance which lingered in the west revealed her; she appeared to him to be standing in a delicate, unearthly halo of luminousness. . . . There was a tear; it hung upon her eyelash as he softly approached her; and when she turned at the sound of his footsteps, it fell upon a white rose which she held to her lips.

It will be observed that the injection of sentiment did not bring new energy to De Forest's prose—quite the contrary. Almost invariably his love scenes put the trite on gaudy display, with images borrowed from the daydreams of inexperienced adolescents. De Forest had never had much success portraying high emotion, but now he felt obliged to try. In later years he explained his repeated, futile, and calamitous attempt. People, he said, "used to ask me why I always had a boy and girl in love in my books, and I used to tell such people that it was the only kind of a plot a writer could get the public interested in."[10]

Although De Forest catered to the public's demand for puerile romance, *Kate Beaumont* was not without redeeming aesthetic value. For example, the author used some very forceful sentences when he described the end of a quarrel between the alcoholic Randolph Armitage and his wife, Nellie (sister of Kate). Awaking after a night of drinking, the still thirsty Randolph discovers that his wife has hidden his remaining liquor. Infuriated, he takes a knife, threatens Nellie with it, demands to know where the bottle is, but is interrupted by the arrival of Kate. Until this point, the scene has been somewhat melodramatic and not entirely convincing: the familiar portrait of a drunkard and his long-suffering wife. Suddenly, however, the clichés fall away, and De Forest provides a chilling view of malice: "'Then I'll leave,' he growled, after a moment's hesitation, meanwhile staring at his knife as if still uncertain whether he would not use it. 'That's all I came here for. Do you suppose I wanted *you?*'"[11] It was not every novelist in Victorian America who had the audacity to write of sexual war—and the skill to compress it into the blade of a knife.

In *Kate Beaumont,* lineage sometimes serves as a mold for stereotyping characters. Because the novel is about a family feud, it naturally calls attention to family resemblances. The McAlisters are persistently grave; the Beaumonts have "warm hearts." Frank McAlister belongs to "an impulsive race"; Nellie Armitage (née Beaumont) has "the quick, effervescent excitability of her Huguenot race." The way membership in a family or ethnic group shaped the behavior of an individual was a preoccupation of De Forest's writings at this phase of his career.[12]

Class also counted. The McAlisters and Beaumonts all come from the higher echelons of society—Frank McAlister even spent eight years studying in Europe. The most aristocratic figure in the book is Colonel Kershaw, Kate's maternal grandfather and the patriarch of the Beaumont clan. Unlike most of his chivalrous relatives, however, Kershaw repudiates the atavistic custom of dueling and says that recourse to the law is a more honorable way of resolving disagreements. Looking like George Washington and speaking with the weight of an oracle, he seems like a god—at least until he is accidentally shot and killed by one of his own reckless and belligerent kinsmen. The fact that the voice of reason comes from a Southern patrician and former high-ranking army officer indicates how aristocratic De Forest's own views were becoming.[13]

De Forest's next three novels were political. *The Wetherel Affair* (published as a book in 1873), *Honest John Vane* (1875), and

Playing the Mischief (1875) all had themes involving politics, sometimes making them the crux of the story, sometimes using them as background, sometimes allowing them to intrude as mere digressions. De Forest focused most frequently on the currently popular subject of graft—these books bubbled up in the wake of the Crédit Mobilier scandal—but he dealt with other current events as well. This concentration on politics was due partly to De Forest's increasingly acute interest in public affairs but was probably also due to his desire to lure readers by discussing fashionable topics.

The Wetherel Affair, which began appearing in the *Galaxy* magazine in December 1872, only three months after the *New York Sun* published its exposé of the Crédit Mobilier, handles politics as a tangent. The novel is essentially a murder mystery with a romance wrapped around it. A man is killed; suspicion falls on his nephew and sole heir; the nephew's fiancée believes him guilty, for she witnessed the crime being committed by someone resembling him; true love is interrupted, and plenteous tears are shed; but, in the end, the murderer is proven to be not the nephew but his look-alike, a Pole named Poloski who claims to be a nobleman. While this plot unravels itself, De Forest (or one of his characters) turns his attention to various political, social, and economic questions. The novel includes arguments against granting the suffrage to immigrants and to people who do not pay taxes; against urban political machines; against strikes by labor unions and against extravagant living by workingmen; against clemency for criminals; and in favor of the profit motive and the capitalists who follow it. This injection of political messages gives De Forest's prose the strangely hollow ponderousness of newspaper editorials, as in this passage that protests the eagerness of American heiresses to marry Europeans with titles:

> One wonders whether the time will ever come when our countrymen will be able to say with unshakeable pride, feeling that there is no loftier boast on earth, "I am an American citizen!" Probably not while our politics remain in their present demagogical chaos. If bosses continue to rule our cities, and old war-horses to neigh brutish stupidities in Congress, it will be well if the entire nation does not follow the example of Alice Dinneford, prostrating itself before some Poloski and saying, "Rule thou over us."[14]

Politics, like romance, had a deadly effect on De Forest's fiction.

Fortunately, some parts of *The Wetherel Affair* are better than others. There are, to the reader's relief, the exuberant monologues of Alice Dinneford, a secondary character who is naughtier than most of De Forest's maidens. Of her uncle, Judge Wetherel, she speaks irreverently, saying that he has a thin, bony frame all cloaked in black, like an umbrella: "I should like to pick him up and open him with a slap, and shut him up again and put him in the umbrella stand." She is even harder on her friend Walter Lehming. Lehming is a hunchback with a head too large for his body, a pious fellow who prays for the patience to endure his deformity, a man of endless self-sacrifice who is always doing good for others. When Alice greets this "incarnation of conscience" (as De Forest calls him), her salutation is remarkable: "'Where have you been these three weeks? I thought you must be dead. I have expected every day to find you decapitated, with your body flopping about like a chicken's, and your head under some policeman's arm, smiling benignantly, as much as to say it was all right and you bore nobody any grudge.'" Alice's speech makes her seem the brightest person in the book, and it comes as a distasteful surprise to be told that she has fallen in love with "Count" Poloski, whom other characters (including Lehming) recognize as a fraud. Plausible characterization is run over by a fast-moving plot.[15]

De Forest's next novel, *Honest John Vane,* devotes itself almost entirely to the question of political corruption, even going so far as to exclude a love story. The tale concerns a small businessman who goes into politics, acquires a reputation for honesty, and, on the basis of that reputation, gets elected to Congress. His political rise, however, only leads to a moral fall, for, once in Washington, he is bribed by "the Ring" to vote subsidies for an immense fraud called the Great Subfluvial Tunnel. (The tunnel probably had as its real-life prototype the Hoosac Tunnel, which in the 1850s was to be blasted through a mountain of rock for the curious purpose of connecting Greenfield, Massachusetts, to the New York state line. Despite considerable cost to Massachusetts taxpayers, the tunnel was never completed.) The message of this polemical novel is obvious, but De Forest states it anyway: "Nothing in the future is more certain than that, if this huge 'special legislation' machine for bribery is not broken up, our Congress will surely and quickly become, what some sad souls claim that it already is, a den of thieves."[16]

Playing the Mischief also makes much of jobbery. Although a love story occasionally appears, the center of attention is the attempt by the young widow Josephine Murray to persuade Congress to pay her a huge and undeserved indemnity for a barn destroyed by American troops during the War of 1812. Josie makes use of her pretty looks and pleasant ways, and eventually she gets a hundred thousand dollars. Whereas the prose of *Honest John Vane* is consistently drab, that of *Playing the Mischief* is merely uneven. De Forest sometimes writes with wit and restraint, as in the book's suggestive first sentence: "Josephine Murray was one of those young women whom every body likes very much on a first acquaintance." At times, however, his writing has the subtlety of a cannon, and considerably less force: "It was the cost, the expenditure, the ostentatious extravagance, which made Josie Murray wet her lips." The book had a certain timeliness and appealed to some people who read newspapers, but only occasionally did it attain the level of literature.[17]

Playing the Mischief continued De Forest's preoccupation with ideas of families and inheritance. For example, a minor character named Griper Jinks has furniture displaying his family's coat of arms, showing that "he has ancestors just about as much as an ape." But while this passage mocks aristocratic pretensions, most of the book praises aristocracy. The Murray family has "godly ancestors and a decent race thus far"; and "the honor of our family" makes them oppose Josie's attempt to defraud the government. Gentility begets integrity.[18]

After exploiting politics for three years and three novels, De Forest turned to something new. Still looking for that elusive quarry, a bonafide best-seller, he now attempted to write the "woman's novel." His next two books, *Justine's Lovers* (1878) and *Irene the Missionary* (1879), were published anonymously. In them, De Forest tried "to imitate the ordinary woman's novel," as he later said, and he wanted readers to think the author was a woman. In this he succeeded. The review for the *New York Post*, for instance, reported that *Justine's Lovers* was "essentially a woman's novel, written by a woman, for women." As imitation female-fiction, the books made little mention of politics, concentrating instead on matters of the heart and the hearth. Perhaps with a sardonic smile, perhaps with a sneer, perhaps with a face straightened by adversity and desperation, De Forest attempted to crowd in amongst the mob of scribbling women. In 1868 he had set out to write the Great American Novel; in 1878 he was writing the Woman's Novel instead.[19]

Of the two woman's novels, *Justine's Lovers* was the better. It contained some excellent passages; for example, the wryly hilarious description of Mrs. Starkenburgh and her illuminated display of family portraits. On the whole, however, the book was not superb. It was afflicted by outbursts of piety—"Depend on it, there are miraculous mercies and inspired soothings in the Bible which can be found nowhere else"—and the engine pulling the plot was not logic but sentiment. In the novel, the wealthy Miss Justine Vane (no relation to Honest John) gets engaged to a handsome, ambitious lawyer named Henry Starkenburgh. She suddenly loses her fortune, he breaks the engagement, she must work to support herself and her widowed mother, but is refused a clerkship by the cold-hearted bureaucrats of the federal government. After wrestling with her conscience, Justine becomes engaged to a rich, middle-aged gentleman for whom she has "profound esteem" but not "passionate adoration." The gentleman dies before the wedding and leaves his fortune to her; Starkenburgh quickly resubmits his proposal of marriage but is turned away. Justine, no longer obliged to marry someone well-to-do, now can marry for love, and conveniently available is a poetry-writing graduate of Yale—which just goes to show that no one has to make a hard choice between love and money, at least not in a woman's novel.[20]

Irene the missionary certainly doesn't have to. In the book laboring under her name, she is courted by three men: an American consul in Syria, a medical missionary, and a rich young gentleman of no particular vocation. Since the last mentioned proves his mettle by rescuing Irene from massacre by heathens, she has no trouble making her choice. The book's main virtue is its description of people and scenes in the Levant; *Irene the Missionary* is not much more than a fictionalized *Oriental Acquaintance.* By combining a love story with an exotic setting, then stirring in a dash of adventure, De Forest returned to a recipe he had followed in *Overland.* This time, however, he added a new ingredient that he thought would make the concoction even more appealing—religion. Just before the novel began serialization in the *Atlantic,* De Forest told editor Howells that "there is a large public which is interested in missions," and he suggested that Howells advertise the novel in religious newspapers.[21]

In 1881 De Forest published *The Bloody Chasm,* a novel that again focused on current events, in this case the reunion of North and South after the Civil War. (The phrase "bloody chasm," referring to the political distance between the two regions, was taken from a speech by Horace Greeley, the liberal Republican who, in his presidential bid of 1872, had promised to bridge the chasm.) De Forest's story is resistant to summary and invulnerable to parody. A Boston millionaire (Silas Mather) has only two possible heirs: a nephew (Harry Underhill), a former Union army colonel, and a niece (Virginia Beaufort), an embittered Charlestonian who has lost all her brothers and all her wealth in the war. Virginia proudly refuses to accept "Yankee dollars" from the philanthropic Mather, so when he dies, he leaves his fortune to Underhill. Mather's will stipulates, however, that if Virginia were to marry Underhill, she would get half the fortune. By now Virginia is desperate for money—not so much for herself as for her aging aunt and her loyal former slaves—so she agrees to the marriage. She insists, though, on one rather large condition: she and Underhill are not to live together (thereby excluding all that "living together" implies—not for nothing is this Carolina girl named Virginia). Underhill, a gentleman, wishes to relieve Virginia's poverty and therefore agrees to the marriage. They are wed in a darkened room, so that Virginia need not even see the face of the hated Yankee vandal, and when the service is over, without so much as a kiss, she collects her inheritance and flees to Paris. Underhill, by this time, has decided that he wants his marriage to be like most people's, so he follows her. Masquerading as a former Confederate officer (Virginia, it will be remembered, has never seen her husband's face), he befriends her, impresses her with his poetry, wins her respect and love, and, finally, reveals his true identity. Virginia forgets her hatred of Northerners, and the two of them commence living together as proper husband and wife.[22]

Such a novel is not easy to take seriously. Its plot, with a couple who always live apart, seems preposterous—at least, until one recollects the peculiar circumstances of De Forest's own marriage. One thing that can be said for *The Bloody Chasm* is that it makes a point. A man tells Underhill, "You are the North incarnate"; Underhill answers, "and my wife is the South." Not every fiction provides so explicit a guide to its own interpretation. The writing in the book is often careless. There are passages in dialogue form, as if for a play, seemingly the author's way of conveying information he does not deem worth the labor of precise exposition. For example:

> *Virginia* (looking up from her writing). "I—can—not live with him."
> *Aunt Chloe* (with arms akimbo). "Is you a grown woman or a baby?"

This effortless sort of writing frequently goes on for pages at a time.[23]

Five years would pass before De Forest would write another novel, and seventeen before he would publish one. After a book like *The Bloody Chasm,* he probably figured it was time to quit. He was disgusted by his own sell-out, his deliberate manufacture of fictions that, though poorly written, brought in more money than good novels would have; and he made no secret of that disgust. After packing *Overland* and *Kate Beaumont* full of sinking ships at sea, he began *The Wetherel Affair* by saying that a steamer from New York, "although freighted with a possible hero and heroine, reached New Haven without misadventure." As introduction to one of *The Bloody Chasm*'s numerous debates over the propriety of marrying for money, he said, "Then the fatiguing dialogue dribbled on once more." In the short story "Jenny Gridley's Concession" (1878), an unhappy writer wants to create "masterpieces" but, instead, produces "mere ephemeralities" because they sell. De Forest's literary conscience was accusing him of betrayal.[24]

Moreover, he began to suspect that, even if he did ignore popular taste and tried to write masterpieces, he would produce ephemeralities. He knew he was a very good writer, but now he faced evidence that he was not quite a great one. Certainly some critics told him so. One of the most forceful critiques of De Forest's work appeared in the *North American Review* as early as 1872. The reviewer, one T. S. Perry, wrote that De Forest did a fine job of depicting various settings in the United States—"the geology, the botany, the ethnography"—but that he could not invent major characters who were plausible and interesting. Ungenerously mocking the author of the 1868 article "The Great American Novel," Perry suggested that De Forest's fiction was definitely American but not particularly great. Equally dispiriting were the reviews published in the *Nation*. That magazine's evaluation of *Kate Beaumont* concurred with T. S. Perry's, likening the novel to "a play in which the scenery is admirably painted, and all the subordinate characters are excellently represented, . . . but the hero and heroine do not come upon the stage." Later Henry James used the pages of the *Nation* to obliterate De Forest. In one critique he said that *Honest John Vane* had "more energy than delicacy"; in another, that the characters and plot of *Playing the Mischief* were far from realistic. To be sure, De Forest received plenty of favorable reviews, especially from William Dean Howells who called him "really the only American novelist." But for someone who wanted to write the Great American Novel, just a few cogent criticisms could bring on despair. Louis Shepard De Forest recalled once seeing his father despondently feed to the fire the manuscript of an entire novel. Since Louis left home for medical studies in Germany in 1880, the burning probably occurred during the previous decade.[25]

If De Forest was not satisfied with his work, neither was the public. *Playing the Mischief* and *Justine's Lovers* had been aimed at a large audience, but hundreds of first editions reposed in a warehouse for years (along with copies of *Miss Ravenel's Conversion*). De Forest was exasperated by the public's failure to buy his books. In *The Wetherel Affair,* the writer Lehming says that, although a talented, hard-working man can make twelve to fifteen hundred dollars a year by writing for the magazines—"more than a common carpenter, and a good deal less than an expert machinist"—he can make almost nothing from the sale of books. *The Wetherel Affair* deplored "the lack of literary culture among the great mass, the overwhelming majority, of the so-called reading public," and it suggested that the way to win over this great mass was by furnishing them with fiction only a little better than they themselves could write. In a letter to Howells six years later, De Forest reiterated the point: "I don't understand why you and I haven't sold monstrously, except on the theory that our novel-reading public is mainly a female or a very juvenile public, & wants something nearer its own mark of intellect & taste, as for instance, 'Helen's Babies' & 'That Husband of Mine.'" It may seem strange to hear sarcastic words like these from a man who was about to publish *Irene the Missionary,* but De Forest had reason for bitterness. When he sold out literature for the sake of lucre, he did not even get a good price. Probably not more, anyway, than fifteen hundred dollars a year.[26]

Another reason for De Forest's abandonment of fiction was his increasing interest in other matters, particularly politics. In 1875 he sailed to England, where he reported, among other things, terrible effects of alcohol on the poor and laboring classes. In 1876 he wrote a letter to the editor of the *Nation,* urging the elevation of General Rutherford B. Hayes to the presidency. Throughout the 1870s, he wrote magazine articles on political subjects such as the Catholic menace, the Turko-Russian war, and military preparedness. Politics invaded several of his novels, and, in a newspaper interview of 1879, De Forest confessed that public affairs had attained supreme importance in his mind. At an age when gray hairs covered his head and had begun to sprinkle his heavy yellow moustache, the novelist reported that literature had lost some of its luster for him. Earlier, he said, "it was my belief that the greatest man was a literary man, or a man of the finest culture. This belief has been shaken. It now is my belief that the man who best manages his fellow men—the great general or the great statesman—is the leading man in the world in regard to ability." It was more important to win a war or an empire for the United States than to write the Great American Novel.[27]

De Forest, it seems, had gone back to the frame of mind he had possessed twenty or thirty years earlier. When he had first begun writing books, he had doubted whether such an enterprise was worthwhile, useful, manly, honorable. Then the Civil War came along, infused him with self-assurance, and inspired him to make writing his vocation. Now, however, he was beset with doubt again. Writing no longer seemed urgent. Why, then, should he continue?

Money, perhaps? One thing that kept De Forest at his desk all through the 1870s was his need to provide for himself, his wife, and his son. Although details of the family budget are hard to come by, the De Forests apparently lived in a genteel fashion. In about 1874 they moved into a handsome, sixteen-room house on Compton Street in New Haven, and they had at least one servant, a cook. Harriet Shepard De Forest had brought some of her family's wealth into the marriage, but she also seems to have brought expensive tastes. On March 29, 1878, however, all that changed. While spending the winter in Charleston with her father and sister, Mrs. De Forest came down with a chill and died within two days. In view of the apparent alienation between De Forest and his wife, her death probably did not cause him much emotional hardship—certainly it did not reduce his literary output in 1878—and it may have relieved him of a financial burden. Her death moreover gave him an inheritance, for Mrs. De Forest left personal property worth more than ten thousand dollars (mostly in stocks, bonds, and notes). She left no will, and her husband (who was administrator for her estate) probably received a large portion of the ten thousand. Thus, after 1878 De Forest had a little more money, a little less to spend it on, and a little less reason to write.[28]

By 1881, then, De Forest had several reasons to stop writing. He had less need for the money it provided, and it was not providing much anyway. To generate just a modest income, he had to grind out hack work, "mere ephemeralities" that often embarrassed him. Of course, now that he had attained a degree of financial security, he could perhaps ignore the great mass of semiliterate readers and could create something truly superb—but, no, it was too late for that. It was thirteen years ago that he had issued his call for a Great American Novel. He was now fifty-five years old and tired, and he sensed that his fiction, like his poetry, lacked some important element of immortality. Then, too, his thoughts had turned away from literature and toward other things: wars and elections, immigrants, alcohol, and woman suffrage. His business as a novelist had not been very rewarding. He had worked at it for three decades but had gotten discouraged and had even gotten careless. Now, finally, he quit. He did not put down the pen suddenly and forever; in the 1880s he tinkered with at least two novels, and he revised his letters and articles about the Civil War and Reconstruction. But his labor now was halfhearted. Literature was a pastime occasionally indulged, but nothing to be taken seriously. De Forest had ceased to be a writer and had become a mere gentleman instead.

The death of Harriet De Forest left her husband in even greater isolation than before. When she had been about, he had sometimes visited her relatives and gone with her to dinners, lectures, and the like. Now, however, he had less cause to go out. In 1880 the *New York Times* reported that although "DE-FOREST, (JOHN WILLIAM)" was "a man of amiable and estimable qualities," he was "little given to society." In 1882 the *Atlantic* invited De Forest to a garden party in honor of Harriet Beecher Stowe; he sent a letter saying that he "put Mrs. Stowe at the head of all living novelists," but he did not attend. In 1883 he wrote to a fellow resident of New Haven and explained that he sent a note because "I don't make calls."[29]

De Forest's withdrawal from society may have been caused in part by his ill health. In 1874 he was suffering from "a sharp turn of neuralgia." Three years later he sought (unsuccessfully) an appointment in the diplomatic corps, partly for "sanitary" reasons. In 1882 he described himself as "a most miserable victim of dyspepsia & the usual medical remedies therefor." De Forest had been a sickly child, then a sickly war veteran, and now he was becoming a sickly old man. He had, however, a long time yet to live.[30]

Chapter 7

American freemen hate an aristocrat.
J. W. De Forest, *Honest John Vane,* 1875

In *Miss Ravenel's Conversion* and other works of his Republican phase, De Forest evinced an uncommon degree of egalitarianism, generosity, and good humor. Although he could never entirely overcome his ingrained, Whiggish sense of belonging to a superior order of men, he learned to find virtue in the "plain people" and to exult in the new birth of freedom then taking place. In the 1870s, however, his political thinking moved in the opposite direction. Replacing the ideal of equality with the ideal of aristocracy, De Forest mocked and berated laborers, mill girls, office workers, parvenus, blacks, immigrants, Catholics, Jews, feminists, and other vulgar upstarts. Although he seems never to have bolted the Republican Party, he became the extremest sort of Mugwump in his alienation from the common people and his distaste for popular rule.[1]

De Forest was writing with indignation, and the result was a good deal of bad fiction. No longer so tolerant of human imperfection, he felt obliged to combat it on every page. He now wrote with a fierce censoriousness that obliterated nuance: the culpable but admirable Colonel John Carter gave way to the simply despicable Honest John Vane. Occasionally De Forest regained his composure, controlled his writing, and produced some memorable prose; but those occasions came too rarely to secure him lasting fame. Had it not been for his earlier work, produced under the intoxification of democracy, he might not be remembered at all.

Perhaps the best indicators of De Forest's growing conservatism were the black characters in his fiction. In the 1860s, De Forest depicted many blacks as ignorant and childish, but he depicted others as brave, responsible, and bright. The race seemed to combine the good and the bad, not entirely unlike the other races of mankind. During the 1870s, however, the portrayal of blacks became almost entirely malign. At their best they were like Aunt Chloe of *The Bloody Chasm* (a virtual reincarnation of Aunt Chloe of *Uncle Tom's Cabin*), who talked common sense to highfalutin masters. Her intelligence, however, was due to the fact that she came from "a brown race of north-middle Africa, far superior in parts and comeliness to the pure negro." De Forest's pure Negroes were quite lacking in comeliness, courage, intellect, and taste. For instance, a runaway slave in "Annie Howard" (1870) was ugly, dirty, and smelly. Though he possessed "some of the finer moral traits of the African race: he was docile, affectionate and loyal," he was also an idiot and a kleptomaniac. (Not by accident, perhaps, this revolting creature was named George, like the heroic fugitive in *Uncle Tom's Cabin*.) A sailor in *The Wetherel Affair* bore a likeness to this character. Exhibiting "that lowly and undeveloped physiognomy which almost surely indicates a southern black," he shambled, grinned, chuckled, rolled his eyes, wriggled spasmodically, and quaked. In *Irene the Missionary,* the sole black character was a gigantic "bellowing brute" with wild eyes and a "silly, brutish expression." When he assaulted a white man, he was beaten to the ground.[2]

De Forest often pictured blacks as animals. "The Duchesne Estate" (1869) featured "one of the antiques and curiosities of the African race, a negro who had not yet ceased to be fractionally a monkey." In the story "The Colored Member" (1872), a black legislator looked like a monkey, and his father resembled an orangutan. A hack driver in *Playing the Mischief* was "a ragged, giggling, skipping young negro, as full of grins, jumps, and whistles, as if he were a mixture of monkey, parrot, and grasshopper"; and the obsequious Uncle Phil of *The Bloody Chasm* had "the cringing expression of a famished dog."[3]

With so low an opinion of blacks, De Forest was not about to champion their cause. In "The Colored Member," published not long after Congress had passed Ku Klux Klan acts to enforce the Fourteenth and Fifteenth amendments, De Forest inveighed against granting full citizenship to the freedmen. In *Justine's Lovers,* a black woman said that white and black children should not play together and that black people had no use for the ballot. Although De Forest supported the Republican presidential ticket in 1876, the former Freedmen's Bureau officer aligned himself with Southern Redeemers by denouncing the "rascality of the carpet-bagger and of his ignorant dupes." In a campaign letter to the *Nation,* he assured foes of Reconstruction that under President Hayes "negro government and misgovernment" would soon cease. The "evil supremacy" remained in only two or three states, he argued, and soon even there "the native-born Anglo-Saxon citizen will rule supreme. . . . The highly-endowed race, the heroic race, the blood race is sure to win."[4]

De Forest gave the expansive, nineteenth-century interpretation to the word *race*: among the less-endowed "races" were Indians, Jews, and Irishmen. In his sundry writings, De Forest portrayed these groups no more flatteringly than blacks. In *Overland,* for instance, the Apaches were "human brutes," and "almost every man and boy was obviously a liar, a thief, and a murderer." Two Jewish shopkeepers turned up in *The Wetherel Affair*—one a "greasy and rancid youngster," the other "an unwholesomely sallow little creature" with "beadlike eyes." Jared Abrams, the subject of the tale "The Man With a Nose Like an Owl" (1872), was a failed haberdasher, a coward, and a sycophant. "Father Higgins's Preferment" was a satire on Catholics in general and the Irish in particular. That story, published in *Harper's,* was so uncharitable that it led the magazine reviewer of the *Nation* to call it "a tale which is neither wise nor witty, and to which we call the attention of the *Catholic World.*"[5]

De Forest did not always believe that ridicule was a strong enough weapon against inferior races. In 1878, as the Russians wound up a successful war against the Turks, De Forest hoped that the czar's military power would clear the infidels from the Bosphorus. "It will be a day of jubilee for Europe," he said in a magazine article, "when the only Asiatic horde remaining on her soil shall be driven forth from it, or at least deprived of all power therein." Urging the Russians to "avenge all the Christian blood which has been poured out upon the track of the Crescent," De Forest rejoiced in the forward march of civilization:

> The noblest of continents freed at last from clownish invasion, and from the blighting influence of a hopelessly barbaric race; the illustrious mother of Aryan men, the chief light and strength and glory of the world, the parent of the highest culture and art and law, delivered altogether to her own incomparable children,—how can the most eloquent tongue or pen do justice to this magnificent hope and possibility?[6]

No longer did De Forest entertain, as he had a decade earlier, any doubt about the superior character and culture of "Aryans."

When not warding off challenges to Anglo-Saxon or Aryan supremacy, De Forest was busy keeping women in their place. One of his favorite targets of satire was the agitator for women's rights. Maria Stanley, who appears in both *Overland* and "Annie Howard," is a feminist (and abolitionist) who is ignorant, credulous, and cowardly. Though she proclaims women mentally and morally superior to men, she frequently demonstrates "woman's need of man's help." She depends on men for financial support, and when some small animals get loose in the room where she sleeps, she screams in terror until rescued by a man. A similar frail reed is "Squire" Nancy Appleyard of *Playing the Mischief.* Though she dresses like a man and wants to practice law, she entirely lacks masculine moral strength. When a crisis occurs, she lapses into hysteria.[7]

De Forest devoted an entire novella to ridiculing the movement for sexual equality. In "Della" (1870), insanity transforms a "sweet, dear child" into a reckless beast. The "disordered child" takes to smoking cigarettes and getting drunk on champagne; she goes to the theater alone and demands gambling halls for women. Feeling "perfect freedom," Della declares that all aspects of life need renovating. "When we come to vote," she warns, "you will see what follows." (De Forest wrote this piece when feminists were demanding that the Fifteenth Amendment be extended to guarantee suffrage for women as well as blacks.)

Unfortunately for the wild girl, however, the madness that frees her from restraint also returns her to it. Falling into a state of catalepsy, followed by an uncontrollable outburst of rage, she is locked up in an asylum. After months of forced rest, she is cured—mentally, at least. Just before dying of pneumonia contracted during her insanity, she repents of her "horrible follies."[8]

Besides depicting feminist derangement, "Della" spells out how a proper lady should behave: "Is a woman fitted for independence? Is a climbing plant fitted to stand alone, or a bee fitted to dispense with the hive? . . . It is not in the nature of the healthy female creature to burst through the environment and reject the regulations of her kind." As long as Della is healthy, she is "a model young lady . . . with the sweetest and purest tone of thought; her conversation more remarkable for good sense than for brilliancy; her modesty so retiring as often to annoy her pushing mother." She is, in short, "a woman nobly suited for a wife." But then she gets a blood clot on her brain, goes berserk, and becomes a feminist.[9]

De Forest made many of his female characters into stiff models of "True Womanhood": emotional, unintellectual, domestic, submissive. Alice Dinneford of *The Wetherel Affair* "was a true woman; in an affair which concerned her sentiments, she was almost ungovernable." Annie Howard—who was "simply a woman"—loved jewelry, hated arguments, and wanted only to have a family. Kate Beaumont was not "altogether womanish"—she was meditative and judicious. Nevertheless, she was domesticated enough to say that "a good cookery-book ought to be the main class-book in every girls' school"; and her sister, Nellie Armitage, agreed, saying that "pudding-making and love-making are woman's chief business." Justine Vane had to be taught by a man that there was such a thing as a chain of reasoning; she could not comprehend either law or science. When she got engaged, her mother advised her that "man's work is more important in his estimation than woman's will" and that a wife must not disagree with her husband over any matter not involving morality. "I shall not quarrel," promised Justine. "I shall obey, mamma, obey!" In *The Bloody Chasm*, the voice of common sense, Aunt Chloe, drew an apt analogy when discussing female fickleness: "Women-folks is like niggers—can't have deir way much in dis yere world; gits along easier if dey *can* change deir minds." Throughout the 1870s, De Forest devoted much of his fiction to the argument that women, like blacks, had better learn their rank in the social order.[10]

If inferior races and the second sex were targets of De Forest's scorn, so too were the common people of any color or gender. De Forest's sense of class superiority—a sense that was keen during his Whig phase but diminished during his Republican phase—now became more intense than ever. Although he still had a few good words for democracy, he could not help viewing the masses as ignorant, foolish, unprincipled, childish at best but often simply depraved. This conviction held true not only for the poor, the very lowest stratum of society, but also for the middling classes of workers and businessmen. (De Forest, who always lived in towns and cities, had little to say about farmers.) As a proper Mugwump, De Forest looked down upon everybody beneath the level of Brahmin.

Contempt for the poor was something he had acquired early and had never given up. In *Seacliff,* for instance, he had described a family of ne'er-do-wells called the Warners. Testy, lazy, and drunken, they were forever bringing unwanted children into the world and whimpering about their bad luck. "The father was a simpleton, the mother a tartar, the children pests to the neighborhood." The Warners bore a close resemblance to the lowdowners De Forest later found in South Carolina. Quarrelsome but also obsequious, the crackers remained sober only because they were too lazy to earn enough money to to buy whiskey. One such family, the Simminses, had been "indigent, ignorant, stupid, and vicious farm-laborers" for centuries, and in all that time their only service to society had been "to drive off the still more worthless Indian."[11]

In "The Great American Novel," De Forest made plain his attitude toward the lowest class. Discussing Rebecca Harding Davis's *Waiting for the Verdict* (1867), a novel dealing melodramatically with the condition of mulattoes in the North, he said:

In reading it we remember with wicked sympathy the expression of a bachelor friend, "I hate poor people's children," and we are tempted to add, "and poor people." We do not believe that "the poor and lowly of God's creatures" are his chosen; we hold that, if he has any preference, it must be for the wisest, sweetest, and noblest. It is dreadful to have low, tattered, piebald, and stupid people so rubbed into one.

It is worth noting that this diatribe against the lowly occurred during De Forest's Republican phase and in an essay honoring the American masses; there was an apparent contradiction between De Forest's hatred of poor people and the generally democratic tenor of his political thought at the time. That contradiction, however, was not as contrary as it seems. The problem with poor people, as De Forest saw it, was that they were lazy, "worthless," unproductive. As such, they stood in marked contrast to the rest of the nation, "this eager and laborious people." As parasites living in a land of producers, the poor were distinctly in the minority; consequently, De Forest did not think of them as part of "the people," but only as a small, corrupt band who stood in opposition to a virtuous general public. De Forest, good Republican that he was, could therefore praise the people and condemn the poor.[12]

That line of thought, however, was in the 1860s. During the following decade, De Forest's disdain spilled over from the indolent minority to the laborious majority. Forgetting the democratic ideas that had previously checked his elitism, he now disparaged the middling classes. In an article published in 1872, he wrote of "the rabble of the city, the artisans, donkey drivers, etc."—not much of a tribute to craftsmen and laborers. The following year, in *The Wetherel Affair,* he described clerks, mechanics, schoolteachers, milliners, and factory girls as being "in feeding" at a cheap restaurant; and he said that they looked at each other in "a dumb, unobtrusive way, like so many sheep or other ruminating animals at pasture." He referred to them as "of the class which must glance at the cost of a dish before ordering it." Equally despised were the "hurried classes" of businessmen who were "so dragged about by the almighty dollar" that they had little time for dining and none for reading.[13]

The Bloody Chasm again revealed De Forest's distaste for

common folk. In that novel, the wealthy Colonel Underhill thinks of marrying the singer Norah Macmorran but is talked out of such folly. His uncle advises him that "she is a decent girl, perhaps, but still a commonplace Irish girl and a Catholic." Commonplace, Irish, Catholic—three indisputable strikes. Virginia Beaufort, the aristocratic heroine of the tale, is only slightly more generous to Norah, calling her "a good, sweet, nice girl, no matter if she is plebeian." Norah herself tells Underhill that "I am only a poor chorister, the daughter of a poor woman. I must remember what I am." Underhill has second thoughts when he realizes that Norah's mother is a washwoman and her sister a serving girl, but what finally turns him away from Norah is a chance meeting with her brother, a policeman. "Good Heavens!" exclaims the gentleman. "This is *too* much." In the end, Underhill marries Virginia, not Norah. When Norah then weds a toadying music teacher of French origins, Virginia says that the couple are "just suited to each other—both Catholics, both musicians." The barrier of class cannot be overcome.[14]

Not even by the nouveaux riches. J. W. De Forest acknowledged that common people sometimes acquired extraordinary wealth, but he doubted that that made them cease to be common. In his Whig days, he had ridiculed the "parvenudity" of the upwardly mobile, and now he returned to the theme. Honest John Vane was "one of those heroes of industry and conquerors of circumstances known as self-made men, whose successes are so full of encouragement to the millions born into mediocrity, and whom, consequently, those millions delight to honor." Vane began by selling refrigerators in Slowburgh, found himself elevated to public office, and ended up selling his vote in Washington. It was obvious that, when confronted with the self-made man, De Forest did not share the respectful point of view of the "millions born into mediocrity."[15]

The viewpoint he shared was that of the few born into gentility. As De Forest aged, the heroes of his fiction came increasingly from the aristocracy, the highest level of birth and wealth. Captain Colburne of *Miss Ravenel's Conversion* had an income of only a thousand dollars a year, and Lieutenant Thurstane of *Overland* had been "poor." But Frank McAlister of *Kate Beaumont* could afford to spend eight years studying abroad and "would one day be rich"; Edward Wetherel of *The Wetherel Affair* squandered a $50,000 patrimony but then inherited half a million more; Colonel Edgar Bradford of *Playing the Mischief* prided himself on being a "gentleman"; Dr. Charles Caswallon of *Justine's Lovers* studied in Paris and Vienna after graduating from Yale; Hubertsen De Vries of *Irene the Missionary* was a "rich and favored youngster" who would later become an army general; and Colonel Harry Edwards Underhill of *The Bloody Chasm* was wealthy even before he inherited a fortune from his uncle, an "old capitalist" named Mather. As lieutenants and captains gave way to colonels and generals, the middle class fell before the rich. To be a hero in one of De Forest's later novels, one had to belong to the leisure class.[16]

In his earlier novels, good family had not guaranteed good behavior. *Seacliff*'s honorable Louis Fitz Hugh had come from a rich old family, but so had the blackmailing Frank Somerville; Captain Colburne of *Miss Ravenel's Conversion* had been a blue blood, but so had Colonel Carter, Madame Larue, and Lieutenant Van Zandt. When De Forest entered his Mugwump phase, however, he began drawing a direct and high correlation between class and virtue. For example, in *Playing the Mischief,* a tale filled with politicians on the take, the few honorable ones bore names like Edgar Bradford, Winthrop Ledyard, and Stuyvesant Clinton. Henry Foster, hero of "The Lauson Tragedy" (1870), exemplified the American aristocrat, priding himself "on being a gentleman in every sense possible to a republican." Because his ancestors had been clergymen and jurists, "he conceived that he belonged to a patrician class, similar to that which Englishmen style 'the untitled nobility,' and that he was bound to exhibit as many chivalrous virtues as if his veins throbbed with the blood of the Black Prince." That being the case, he was obliged to be brave, honest, fair, generous, and courteous, "not only out of good instincts toward others, but out of respect for himself." Similarly, Edward Wetherel, who stemmed from a line of "Puritans of good social position and of high breeding," had "a sort of conscience" whose main strength lay not in obedience to God but "in self-respect and respect for the name of Wetherel." When Edward was accused of murder, one of his friends reasoned (correctly) that homicide was beneath Edward's dignity: "He was a gentleman; he could not murder." Thus, in De Forest's later fiction, membership in the aristocracy practically guaranteed morality.[17]

Nonmembership did the opposite. To begin with, De Forest argued that the lack of money was the root of much evil. In *Honest John Vane,* for example, the corrupted ex-preacher Greatheart says sadly that none but the rich should hold public office. "A poor fellow *will* get into debt," he says, "and then the lobby offers to help him out, and it is very hard to refuse"—exactly what happens in the novel. Vane, whose modest savings and salary are squandered by his wife (another of De Forest's extravagant females), cannot refuse bribes offered by "the Ring." In contrast stand wellborn men like Colonel Murray of *Playing the Mischief.* Taking pride in his family's long history of rectitude, the colonel reflects that their inherited wealth probably helped to preserve them from "low greed and dishonesty." The fortune-hunting Josie Murray might seem to contradict this stereotype, but she *married* into the family and had no fortune of her own; she was more like the Vanes than the Murrays. De Forest thus shows that the common people are less able to afford honor than are the elite.[18]

There is more involved, however, than mere dollars. Even when reduced in fortune, De Forest's aristocrats rarely stoop to folly: their self-respect keeps them from it. The wellborn but impoverished heroine of *Justine's Lovers,* for example, does nothing more dishonorable than apply for a government job, and her fastidious conscience torments her even for accepting the marriage proposal of a rich man whom she respects but does not quite love. Boors like Honest John Vane, unfortunately, have no such scruples to protect them:

> There is rabble in morals as well as in manners, and to this spiritual mobocracy Vane belonged by birth. The fibre of his soul was coarse, and it had never been refined or purified by good breeding, and very likely it was not capable of taking a finish. . . . It is impossible to insist too strongly that he had no sound self-respect and lofty sense of honor.

The self-made man has no self-respect: that is reserved for born gentlemen.[19]

Born gentlemen—the fact that Vane belonged to the rabble "by birth" suggests a new element in De Forest's social thought: biological determinism. In the 1860s, De Forest believed that "a man's chances go very far toward making up the actual man," and in the 1870s he sometimes still acknowledged the influence of environment upon character. In *Kate Beaumont,* for example, he said that the Beaumont clan's pugnacity was the result of a centuries-long "education of blood and iron." More often, however, De Forest now stressed heredity, not education, as the prime determinant of behavior.[20]

In "The Russians on the Bosphorus," for example, he said that, despite five centuries of contact, the Aryans and the Ottomans had learned nothing from one another. "One is tempted to infer," he inferred, "that ethnic differences reach deeper than the shape and color of man; that they must be ingrained for all time in his moral and intellectual nature." In his fiction, De Forest illustrated the genetic transfer of moral and intellectual qualities. In *Overland,* Lieutenant Thurstane enjoyed seeing the Grand Canyon because he was "gifted with much of the sympathy of the great Teutonic race for nature." The lieutenant, who also possessed "the earnest sentimentality of the great Teutonic race," was too serious-minded to flirt with ladies; but that was all right with Clara Muñoz Garcia Van Diemen, for although her mother was Mexican, "Clara was half Teutonic, and could comprehend the tone of her father's race." Naturally she preferred the companionship of Lieutenant Thurstane to that of the "mercurial Mexican" Carlos Coronado. Nor was it only Mexicans who lacked the natural virtues of the great Teutonic race. In the story "Yesebel" (1876), a heathen girl was converted to Christianity, behaved well for a while, but eventually reverted to paganism, "as if descended instincts, hereditary impulses, had triumphed over surroundings." A superstitious minister ascribed Yesebel's backsliding to God's will, but a rationalist apothecary was more convincing when he said, "Blood will tell."[21]

Heredity is not only racial; it is also familial. In his Mugwump fiction, De Forest shows how character traits are passed down in a lineage. Edward Wetherel, for example, starts out as a young man of impeccable old family but "half a pagan in education and almost wholly pagan in soul." After his uncle is murdered, however, Edward turns over a new leaf and becomes "a decent, serious, fairly able and hard-working young man." This change is exactly the opposite of Yesebel's, but has exactly the same cause: "a new soul has been born. Not a new one, either; it is the grave, earnest soul of the Wetherels; it is the resurrection of his Puritan ancestors." De Forest was fond of what he called the "ethnological explanation," and he elaborated it in later novels. In *Playing the Mischief,* he said that "we are our ancestors over again," then continued, "One may say that there is never a new, a perfectly individual temperament born upon earth. Circumstances and education vary the transmitted type more or less in exteriors, but not at all in its inner character." No wonder the soul of Honest John Vane was incapable of refinement.[22]

In *Justine's Lovers,* De Forest exposed the scientific basis of his hereditarian social thought. Ralph Starkenburgh, a minor character in the novel, is an upright, able, and generous old man, and he offers some advice: "'Have you read Galton's "Hereditary Descent of Genius'"? No? You should read it. It is a great and terrible revelation. We are the sons of our fathers, and not of our own little resolves." De Forest's biological determinism seems to derive from the English scientist Sir Francis Galton.[23]

Galton (1822–1911) was a cousin of Charles Darwin and a man of perilously long vision. The inventor of the word *eugenics,* he advocated the careful breeding of "a highly gifted race of men by judicious marriages during several consecutive generations"—a project that would kindly allow "the weak" to "find a welcome and a refuge in celibate monasteries or sisterhoods." The success of such a eugenic enterprise would depend on the truth of one assumption—"that a man's natural abilities are derived by inheritance." If natural abilities were not hereditary but were distributed randomly throughout the population, then of course it would be impossible to breed a "highly gifted race." *Hereditary Genius* (1869), the book to which Ralph Starkenburgh referred, was intended to prove that heredity, not chance, was at work. The book's aim, however, was limited. It did *not* attempt to prove that "natural abilities" were the only abilities that mattered, that "circumstances and education" made no changes in one's "inner character," or that human "resolves" meant "little." De Forest, however, did not notice these omissions. He believed Galton proved scientifically that "we are our ancestors over again"—so much for the self-made man.[24]

Believing in the natural superiority of gentlemen, De Forest found a great deal that was unnatural in the America of the 1870s. Though the aristocrats excelled in culture, intellect, and morals, they had been bested in politics. Again and again De Forest inveighed against the "demagogical chaos" engendered by granting the franchise to immigrants and to men without property. He bewailed the tyranny of political bosses, and he particularly assailed New York City, which he called a "sink of undisturbed lawlessness." Contemplating "the vast morasses and Pontine marshes of undrained, uncleared crime, which send up their horrible malaria on the island of Manhattan," he lamented that the city's police were "models either of eminent dishonesty or eminent incapacity." The inadequacy of New York's Finest had an obvious cause: "A people which suffers itself to be ruled politically by its non-taxpayers . . . must necessarily have inferior magistrates and officers."[25]

Lawlessness was not the only "chaos" bred by democracy. Even more ominous was economic disorder. In a democracy, De Forest believed, ideas of equality make everyone want to live as splendidly as anyone else. People of small means envy the rich and long to "wallow in luxury." In the short run, this desire leads the laboring classes to impoverish themselves by being "absurdly and ruinously extravagant." In the long run, it leads them to rebel against the rich. Artisans and workingmen do not realize that "the raising of wages involves the raising of expenses" and that "what they need is not higher pay, but cheaper living." Because of this ignorance of political economy, they do all sorts of foolish and dangerous things—like blaming capitalists for the problems of workers and like going on strike. In *The Wetherel Affair,* De

Forest asks the big question: "Will democracy destroy us?" In his next novel, he suggests an answer.[26]

Honest John Vane is a denunciation not only of political corruption but also, more fundamentally, of the democracy that seemed to De Forest to make such corruption inevitable. Running for Congress against a gentleman who has the misfortune of bearing the illustrious name Saltonstall, John Vane wins the election because "American freemen hate an aristocrat" and prefer to be governed by ordinary men like themselves. The "great majority" of the voters do not suppose that their representative needs any more intelligence or integrity than that needed to vote the party line. The few wise men who believe that a legislator ought to know something about politics, economics, and law, and that he should be of proven character—these few have no political influence. The government is in the hands of the mob.[27]

Honest John Vane, a typical work of De Forest's Mugwump period, had some things in common with *Miss Ravenel's Conversion*, the masterpiece of his Republican phase—namely, a similarity of plot and a shared allusion to John Bunyan. Miss Ravenel's conversion from secession (and slavery) to loyalty (and equality) was patterned after the Pilgrim's progress from this world to that which is to come. The story of John Vane abandoning his honesty was (as De Forest described it) "a reversed and altogether bedeviled rendering of the Pilgrim's Progress." Both novels portrayed democracy. The only difference was that, while *Miss Ravenel's Conversion* showed it as a success that produced noblemen of nature, *Honest John Vane* showed it as a failure that produced venal politicians. The later book demonstrated the novelist's loss of faith in popular rule, the people, and nineteenth-century America—De Forest's conversion from loyalty to secession.[28]

As a rebel against democracy, De Forest had lots of company, at least in polite society, Cambridge, and the *Nation*. In the decades after the Civil War, a corps of eloquent intellectuals deplored what they viewed as the rise of democracy and the decline of gentility. Henry Adams wrote a novel about corruption and entitled it *Democracy*, and he spent the rest of his life questioning the virtue of a republic that chose to be led by a Grant instead of an Adams. Charles Eliot Norton of Harvard blamed democracy for a national "decline of manners." E. L. Godkin, editor of the *Nation,* denounced immigrants, satirized self-made men, complained that "avarice" had overthrown "plain living and high thinking," blamed imperialism on popular rule, proposed that rich men be allowed more votes than common ones, and, in a final gesture of disgust, removed himself to the more aristocratic purlieus of England. Among men of this sort, De Forest's Mugwump ideas were not iconoclastic.[29]

Of course, the critique of democracy was nothing entirely new. Throughout the nineteenth century—as early as Hugh Henry Brackenridge's *Modern Chivalry* (1792–1805)—commentators had perceived a decline of standards in the country. James Fenimore Cooper scorned Americans' commercialism and their relentless drive toward mediocrity. Alexis de Tocqueville regretted that, in a nation of equals, heroic character and delicate taste were lost. In the nostalgic moods of his Whig phase, J. W. De Forest had also lamented the demise of ancient, aristocratic virtues. What was new in the writings after the Civil War was not the insistence that democracy had disadvantages, but the denial that it had advantages that more than compensated. For all their criticisms of democracy, men like Brackenridge, Cooper, de Tocqueville, and the early De Forest had insisted that it was the most just and humane form of society. What was said of Cooper might have been said of any of them: he was "an aristocrat in feeling, and a democrat by conviction." In the late nineteenth century, however, the conviction was changing, at least among one very articulate segment of the upper class. There was a suspicion that the rise of the masses was a disaster with little mitigation, if any. Nostalgia was hardening into genuine grief.[30]

The critique of democracy had two focal points: morals and manners. In regard to morals, Mugwumps believed that the masses were less motivated by principles than were the social elite. In 1869 Henry Adams published an article comparing two members of President Grant's cabinet: George Boutwell, "the product of caucuses and party promotion," and Ebenezer Hoar, "by birth and training a representative of the best New England school, holding his moral rules on the sole authority of his own conscience." The common man did what was popular; the gentleman did what was right. In his novel *Democracy,* published eleven years later, Adams showed what happened when the Boutwells supplanted the Hoars: "The old is going; the new is coming. Wealth, office, power are at auction. Who bids highest? who hates with most venom? who intrigues with most skill? Who has done the dirtiest, the meanest, the darkest, and the most political work? He shall have his reward"—shades of *Honest John Vane.*[31]

As for manners, the critique was equally severe. In the late nineteenth century, more than ever before, the well-to-do began to treasure leisure, decorum, and taste and to abhor the artless existence of the toiling classes. This growing gentility was particularly evident in Boston, which had once been the nation's business center but which now, since the rise of Philadelphia and New York, had to console itself with being the hub of the universe. Before the Civil War, Boston Brahmins had admired commercial achievements so much that William H. Prescott could refer without irony to "the noble post of head of a cotton factory." After the war, though, Brahmins like Francis Parkman, Brooks and Henry Adams, and Richard Henry Dana Jr. condemned commerce and industry as "vulgar." Nathan Appleton (born 1779) had made a fortune in business and had taken pride in his calling, but his son Thomas (born 1812) deplored the pursuit of wealth and considered himself a worshipper of beauty. William Dean Howells depicted the transformation of values in his novel *The Rise of Silas Lapham* (1885). Bromfield Corey's father had grown rich in the India trade, but Bromfield—who is horrified to discover that the parvenu Lapham drinks ice water instead of wine—prides himself on doing nothing.[32]

If Bromfield Corey had actually lived, he might have been an exact contemporary of J. W. De Forest, and the two men were remarkably similar in careers and ideas. De Forest's father, like Corey's, had engaged in business; John Hancock De Forest had held, in fact, what Prescott called "the noble post of head of a cotton factory." John William, like Bromfield, traveled for years in Europe, refined his tastes, gave himself over to the fine arts (painting for Corey, writing for De Forest), and never made much money. Finally, De Forest despised the crassness of John Vane just as Corey despised the crassness of Silas Lapham. In the fictional and actual worlds of the late nineteenth century, gentlemen cultivated a keen distaste for people who did not fit into what Corey called "the airy, graceful, winning superstructure" of society.[33]

In one final respect De Forest exemplified an elitist strain of social thought in post-bellum America—his belief that all the crucial elements of character were inherited, not learned, that "we are our ancestors over again." Early in the century, Hugh Henry Brackenridge, though saying that politics ought to be left to the educated, had also said that "pedigree" did not determine ability. Sages often had blockheads for sons, he said, and the odds were a hundred to one against any descendant of Jefferson or John Adams being able to take his place—the "brat of a tinker" was more likely to be a "man of genius." James Fenimore Cooper, while attributing superior "gifts" to gentlemen, had said that those gifts came from lifelong association with other gentlemen, that is, from training. "Breeding" was a matter of culture, not biology. By the end of the nineteenth century, social theory had changed. Brooks Adams declared in 1893 that mental characteristics were passed down through the blood. The reason for a family's success in one century but not in the next (and one can guess which family Adams had most in mind) was not because the later generations had degenerated, but because changes in society had decreased the family's opportunities to act. What was true of families was also true of nations. Adams and many other scholars of the period maintained that different "races" had different natural aptitudes. When De Forest said that Anglo-Saxons were inherently more intelligent and courageous than other ethnic groups, he was only agreeing with many of the sages of contemporary social science.[34]

The strength (or at least the abundance) of extreme anti-democratic ideas was a distinctive feature of the last decades of the century. People like the Adams brothers believed that most other people had low morals and bad manners, and that nothing else could be expected of commonplace families and inferior races. What was being conducted in the journals, universities, and elite social clubs was a revolt against democracy; a rise of American gentility. In such books as *The Wetherel Affair* and *Honest John Vane,* J. W. De Forest participated in that uprising.

De Forest adored the genteel and despised the common, and that combination of prejudices guided his fiction into the stiff territory of the ideal. His heroines and heroes had always had a certain porcelain quality, like figurines representing virtue, but some of his other characters had possessed complications, contradictions, small surprises that had made them interesting and alive. Now, however, almost every character seemed to be an idea on two legs, an incarnation of the precious or the base. Self-made men cheated; born gentlemen did not. Anglo-Saxon men faced up to danger; Mexicans and women hid. There were no more individuals; there were only types.

In his political novels, De Forest proved especially ready to resort to types. *Honest John Vane* was a full-fledged allegory, *Pilgrim's Progress* in reverse. *Playing the Mischief* was more realistic, but only slightly. In portraying a corrupt Congressman, for example, De Forest showed a heavy hand: "'We are not representatives of the people at all,' laughed Drummond. 'We are representatives of the wire-pullers and log-rollers who run the primary meetings.'" De Forest was more intent on indicting criminals than on scrupulously reproducing their actions and words. As Henry James pointed out in his review of *Playing the Mischief,* "the barefaced candor with which the conspirators talk their fraudulent designs over with one another is, we should say, improbable even in these days. . . . Mr. De Forest has a great deal of cleverness, but he overdoes his 'realism.'"[35]

Of course, much of De Forest's writing of the 1870s had merit (James acknowledged his "cleverness"), but even his best passages were often distorted by political convictions. For example, *Justine's Lovers* contains an amusing description of a kindergarten, a swirl of adventure and petty violence. The charm of the scene is dissipated, however, when one child, the daughter of an abolitionist, declares that she does not want to play with black children. Asked what her father would think of such a refusal, she replies that it is right to campaign in behalf of colored people but wrong to play with them. Somehow this hairsplitting argument for segregation does not seem the work of a kindergartner. De Forest, however, is willing to jettison plausibility to convey a message.[36]

A similar violation of fiction occurs in *Playing the Mischief,* though with results not quite so disastrous. One of the book's most entertaining scenes is a confrontation between the fortune hunter Josie Murray and the feminist Nancy Appleyard, both of whom have eyes on the handsome Congressman Drummond. "Squire" Nancy addresses her rival:

> "Mrs. Murray, I am a druggist as well as a lawyer," and by this time her voice was so hoarse and sepulchral as to be terrible, at least to Josie. "I am a druggist. I have here two pills made by myself. One of them is bread, and the other is arsenic. They shall decide between us. Take your choice, and I will take the other. The survivor shall have Sykes Drummond. The other," and here her utterance fell to a hoarse murmur which would have been fatal to a sensitive listener—"the other *d-i-e-s!*"
>
> It must have been wonderful to see her poking her prescription at Mrs. Murray, and that lovely young person recoiling from it. For there is no doubt that she did recoil, and that she was at this moment considerably flustered. Indeed, if we may believe Squire Nancy's subsequent description of the scene, Josie shed tears, babyishly, and said, in a contemptible whisper, "I can't take pills without jam."
>
> Our heroine, however, always denied the alleged weeping, and gave a much nobler version of her refusal to swallow. According to her account, she only said, "I can't take dry pills," and said it, too, in a tone of cutting irony.
>
> Indeed, the discrepancies of statement between the two ladies with regard to this whole interview, are simply irreconcilable.[37]

This passage is De Forest at his best. Josie's revulsion is palpable, the divergent accounts of her behavior provide sudden glimpses into two different worlds, and only the most serious-minded reader can resist a smile. Still, even here, there is something amiss. Even if one does not resent the depiction of a feminist as a man-hungry fool, one must notice that Nancy Appleyard is grotesque, hyperbolic; her histrionics are not quite believable. While Josie seems like a human being, Nancy seems like a cartoon. The juxtaposition of two such incongruous characters accounts for much of the humor of the scene, but it exacts a high price—it sacrifices credibility. Once again De Forest's political prejudices have led him into caricature; his fiction and his politics could not coexist.

Chapter 8

Unrecorded he died, perhaps with a bitter sense
of having failed in life, as has happened to many
whom earth will never forget.

J. W. De Forest, The De Forests of Avesnes, 1900

The last quarter of De Forest's life consisted mainly of irritation and pain. He was sick, as always. His "old war exposures" nearly killed him during the winter of 1885–1886, and in 1893 he was placed in a hospital for treatment of influenza. Also, as always, he was short of cash. In 1885 he advised his son to terminate his medical studies, for funds were low; in the 1890s he began petitioning the government for a Civil War pension; in 1904 he was awarded the pension—twelve dollars a month. What may have kept him solvent during these last lean years was the timely death of a relative. In 1888 the mathematician Erastus Lyman De Forest died and left his cousin a sum called "substantial" by the novelist's son and estimated at twenty thousand dollars by his grandson. Whatever its size, the inheritance did not elevate De Forest into luxury. In the 1890s, he lived in one room of a hotel near the railroad station. It was a solitary life. He lived alone, and he had never been fond of visiting.[1]

Privacy, however, was not peace. De Forest's last years were filled with a turbulence of the spirit, with prolonged brooding on troubles both personal and political. Why had he not achieved fame? How could a man who had published a well-received book at age twenty-five, who had worked at his craft for thirty years, who had written such a fiction as *Kate Beaumont* and won Howells's acclaim, a man of intellect and courage, breeding and resolve—how could such a man have failed? Why had his books gone unsold? Why had he fallen so quickly and completely into obscurity? Why had riches not gone to a man of understanding, nor favor to a man of skill? What had gone wrong? There were several reasons, of course, but one fundamental one—the judgment of the reading public. To J. W. De Forest, that misjudgment provided just one more argument aganst democracy.

De Forest vented his rancor toward the public when he wrote to other men of letters. In 1883, for example, he wrote to T. R. Lounsbury, who had just published a biography of James Fenimore Cooper. After applauding Lounsbury's assertion that the absence of an international copyright law had retarded the developoment of an American literature—an assertion De Forest himself had made fifteen years earlier in "The Great American Novel"—De Forest went on to denounce readers who would rather buy a pirated edition by a European author than pay a few cents more for a copyrighted book by an American. After deploring the selfishness of publishers, he moved on to a bigger target: "The nation at large has been full of dishonesty & meanness; the whole public wants to steal books and plunder authors. . . . I must admit that it behaves like a low-born rabble of Philistines." Besides plundering authors, however, the public did something even more philistine: it ignored them. In a letter of 1886 that pulsed with invective, De Forest told William Dean Howells of his "profound contempt for the great majority of our novel-reading public." The main source of this contempt was not hard to discover. "I know very well," De Forest said, "that I have written a good novel or two, & that out of 50 000 000 Americans not 10 000 have been aware of it." De Forest did not believe he had received the acclaim he had earned.[2]

The letter to Howells made it clear, however, that the mistreatment of authors was not the only failing of the American people but was merely one indication of their general inadequacy. De Forest wrote the letter to congratulate Howells on the serial publication of his novel *The Minister's Charge: or the Apprenticeship of Lemuel Barker.* That book, about a farm boy who seeks his fortune in the city, depicts sympathetically the emotional pain and moral peril of upward mobility. Although Barker fails as a poet and ends up as a country schoolteacher, Howells presents advancement in society as a worthy and feasible goal. The aristocrat Bromfield Corey (who is more egalitarian in this book than in *The Rise of Silas Lapham*) admires Barker's ability, predicts that he will found a family and a fortune, and says with a tone of approval that half of today's Brahmins are descendants of farmers, mechanics, and the like.[3]

When De Forest read the novel, however, he missed entirely Howell's sympathy for Barker and others on the make. Congratulating Howells on "exposing to view the base metal & coarse clay of which nearly the whole American people is fabricated," he described Barker as endowed with some genius but as "a kind of fool," with "an original lack of refinement of soul." Ignoring the rise (if such it were) of Lemuel Barker from farmer to schoolteacher, and ignoring also Corey's prediction of future distinction. De Forest said it was impossible for Barker to go "above his birthline." The "mass of vulgar-born people," he said, are bound to "fizzle out." Among that fizzling mass he located the two working girls Barker met, Monda Grier and Stira Dudley. These two, whom Howells portrayed as interesting and in some ways charming young women, De Forest saw as "masterpieces of born, unfathomable 'lowness,' incurably commonplace." De Forest, in a pathological reading of the novel, called it a revelation of "the vulgarity of plebeianism." Judging, perhaps, from his own experiences, he doubted that *The Minister's Charge* would succeed with the public. "How," he asked, "can salesladies & commercial gents favor a book which reveals their generally unenlargeable littleness of soul?"[4]

Despite his revulsion from plebeians, De Forest had a sort of scientific curiosity about them. He studied different specimens of the common people and was fascinated, like a boy goggling at spiders. In 1881, for example, he began investigating the species known as Catholics. He enjoyed reading a book of poems by one Katherine E. Conway because "they showed a kind of life that I knew little about, & had lately been trying to guess at. There are 4000000 of Catholics in the United States, & this is the first book that I have seen from one of them!" It was unfortunate, however, if De Forest relied on such a book to inform him about the kind of life that four million Catholics led. Miss Conway, the daughter of a "once wealthy" resident of upstate New York, had nothing to say about family life, work, politics, immigration, or the city but wrote instead of "The First Red Leaf" and "Ferns from Watkins Glen." Some of her verses seemed to deal with religious subjects, but they did not sound the profoundest depths of the Roman theology and faith. For instance, the poem with the promising title "Magdalene" begins this way—

> I had no share of the Christmas cheer.
> Nobody wished me a happy New Year

—then goes on to say that Jesus takes pity on the sorrowful. If verses like these struck De Forest with the force of revelation, it said something about his knowledge of Catholics.[5]

In 1886 De Forest's study of the common people was sufficiently complete for him to write a book about them. In 1886 he offered for serialization in magazines a novel called "A Daughter of Toil:—One of the Romances of Working Life." He told the editors of the *Century* that the novel was a real-life story of a "poor & good girl, who by dint of worth & favoring chances, struggles up to—the best she can get"; and in a letter to Howells, who now was writing for *Harper's,* he said that the tale dealt with such subjects as wage scales, the cost of living, details of labor, and housing. Not that the book was realistic. Its plot, said De Forest, "partakes of the nature of romance." Since the novel was completed in the same year in which De Forest described Monda Grier and Stira Dudley as masterpieces of unfathomable lowness, it is doubtful that he could portray his own working woman with the sympathy required for realism.[6]

In any case, neither the *Century* nor *Harper's* nor anyone else would publish the novel. Since De Forest apparently destroyed the manuscript, the only record of it lies in his letters describing it. In 1887 he offered the *Century* another manuscript, one which he said pleased him much better. No magazine published this one either; but, with the help of Howells, De Forest eventually brought it out in book form—in 1898.[7]

In *A Lover's Revolt*, a tale of the eternal triangle set during the American Revolution, De Forest repeated his philippics against contemporary civilization. He portrayed a hideous, sadistic black man and a female social climber. Saying that, in the Revolutionary army, officers were of a higher social class than the rank and file, he observed sardonically that Americans had not yet discovered that people without property were fit to rule those who had it. Saying that the British army consisted almost entirely of Irish, Scotch, and German mercenaries, he maintained that Englishmen would not fight against the cause of liberty. Meanwhile, in "the thirteen Anglo-Saxon colonies," most Americans, "more especially those of pure English descent," rose up against tyranny. Oddly enough, in a war between England and America, America represented the Anglo-Saxons.[8]

A Lover's Revolt suffered from the usual shortcomings of De Forest's later fiction. Characters were caricatures representing a type, a class, or a cause. Patriot Captain Ash Farnlee was tall, muscular, steady, and brave, while loyalist Uncle Fenn had "fawning old teeth" in his "bootlicking mouth." Nationalist exhortation was so relentless that even William Dean Howells, who praised the book for its realism, found it "a little too thumpingly patriotic for my pleasure." Also, as happened in so much of De Forest's writing, sentiment overflowed. Huldah, the heroine, "began to cry, resting her elbows on her knees, supporting her forehead on her hands, and letting the tears drop, drop, drop on the floor."[9]

But the novel also contained some of De Forest's better prose. For example, when brawny Sister Ann broke down in tears, "the men stared at her in a perplexed, discomforted way, as men usually stare at a woman crying, when they don't want to kiss her." De Forest's description of the British retreat from Concord was as plainly truthful as the battle scenes of *Miss Ravenel's Conversion:*

Every few minutes a ball, or perhaps several, hissed spitefully between the files, or struck with that cruel, sickening *chuck* which the veteran knows so well. Then a man uttered a scream, or a groan, and dropped like a sack; or he reeled against some comrade and was helped forward a few steps, soon to be laid by the roadside and left there panting and turning white. . . . Each man who saw another hit felt a sort of gladness because that bullet at least had missed himself.[10]

Sadly, when De Forest was at his very best now, he wrote the way he had written two decades before.

In the 1880s and 1890s, moreover, he was not writing very much at all. In 1883 Thomas Bailey Aldrich suggested to De Forest that the time was right for another novel from him; but, confessing that his mind had turned to other things, De Forest said he had no novel on hand nor even in his head. He would not write another one for at least a year or two, he said, and perhaps never. He did, of course, bestir himself to produce "A Daughter of Toil" and *A Lover's Revolt,* but neither of these books had much success, which was discouraging. In 1890 De Forest told Howells that he was neither writing nor trying to publish. "My mind is drying up," he said, "& I do almost nothing but read, especially in ethnology & other kindred dry matter." In 1898 he told the *New York Times* that he no longer worked on fiction but on ethnology.[11]

One of the ethnological problems that absorbed De Forest's attention was the question of where on the globe humankind first appeared. In an article of 1878, he tried to demolish the old notion that Asia was "The Cradle of the Human Race"—that people originated in India, Afghanistan, or some other part of Asia, then migrated to Europe. Relying on ancient European literature and legend, which made no mention of a migration from the east, De Forest argued that the origin of Europeans was "autochthonous": Aryans were a native product, not an import. Some Europeans then migrated eastward, De Forest said, spreading Aryan languages and civilization to some of the peoples of Asia; thus, although Asia owed something to Europe, the reverse was not true.[12]

In 1890 De Forest returned to this theme. The English clergyman and philologist Isaac Taylor had just published *The Origin of the Aryans: An Account of the Prehistoric Ethnology and Civ-*

ilisation of Europe, which held that the Aryans originated in western Europe. The recent archaeological scholarship, Taylor said, had demonstrated that "the present inhabitants of Spain, France, Denmark, Germany, and Britain are to a great extent the descendants of those rude savages who occupied the same regions in neolithic or possibly in paleolithic times." When De Forest read this statement, he was ecstatic, for although Taylor did not know of De Forest's "The Cradle of the Human Race," he did confirm its conclusions. With some glee, De Forest wrote to the *Nation, Popular Science Monthly,* the *Atlantic,* and William Dean Howells, asking them all to review *The Origin of the Aryans.*[13]

It is not hard to guess why De Forest was pleased. First, Taylor's work seemed to free Aryans of any Asiatic antecedents; De Forest probably did not want to think of himself as a cousin of Turks and Chinamen. Second, Taylor made De Forest look like a prophet. In his letter asking Howells to review the book, De Forest said that he was delighted to discover that his 1878 article had been "wise" and that he had been one of the first in America to understand the subject. After Howells dutifully wrote a review, which praised De Forest as well as Taylor, De Forest replied with a note of thanks. "Observe," he said, "that this is the first time that I have been mentioned in my own country, in connection with an article which would have been remarked, & almost important, in any other country, barring cannibaldom." For once, though twelve years late, he had gotten the recognition he deserved.[14]

De Forest welcomed his rare moments in the limelight. In 1898, after Howells had persuaded a publisher to put out *A Lover's Revolt,* De Forest thanked him for "your most friendly and useful interference to draw me from the obscurity into which I had fallen." The book's publication brought De Forest to the attention of the *New York Times,* which sent a reporter to interview the rediscovered author. According to the resulting article, De Forest was "full of anecdotes of his youth and of his long and hard struggle to win fame and the pleasure of it when he reached it." In 1899 the first volume of *Who's Who in America* appeared, and De Forest ordered a copy. He probably did so with considerable pleasure, for one of the notables listed was "DE FOREST, John William, author."[15]

But the "long and hard struggle to win fame" was not over yet. If De Forest had ever reached that splendid goal, he had subsequently strayed from it. After 1881, when he had pretty much given up on writing novels, De Forest had to find other ways to get a hold on immortality. One way—exemplified by his letter-writing campaign regarding the cradle of the human race—was to return attention to what he had done and written previously. In the 1880s, he went back to his articles of the 1860s and attempted to have them published between hard covers. He collected his pieces on the Civil War, revised them, added excerpts from letters he had written to his wife during the war, called the manuscript "Military Life," and, around 1890, rewrote the whole thing and called it "A Volunteer's Adventures." Also during the 1880s he assembled and revised his articles on Reconstruction, calling that manuscript "The Bureau Major." He was not bashful when he depicted his career. In the autobiographical preface to his war narrative he reported that his commanding general had called him "one of the best volunteer officers that I ever had under me." Unfortunately, though, these pleasant words did not reach the public while De Forest was alive. His two manuscripts were not published until James Croushore and David Potter resurrected them after the Second World War.[16]

Besides collecting old articles, De Forest tried to reissue old books. As early as 1878 he had apparently thought of publishing a collection of his novels, for the short story "Jenny Gridley's Concession" involved a writer who was unhappy because he could not get out a "library edition" of his books. By 1884, when De Forest was not certain he would ever write another novel, he tried hard to find a publisher for a standard edition. Having obtained the rights to *Kate Beaumont, Overland,* and *The Wetherel Affair,* he wrote to Harper and Brothers, who owned the plates and copyright to *Miss Ravenel's Conversion, Justine's Lovers,* and *Playing the Mischief.* Maintaining that all the novels would sell better if produced in a uniform edition, he asked Harpers if they would like to sponsor such a project. Harpers diplomatically replied that the idea was a good one but that, unfortunately, they had too many engagements to think of carrying it out. To enable De Forest to do so, however, they generously offered to sell him the plates at half cost—"on the understanding that you or your publisher would at the same time purchase, at cost, the copies of these books which we have on hand." Since Harpers had in stock more than three thousand copies of the three novels, the price would have been formidable. Moreover, as if to add insult to injury, Harpers suggested that De Forest, while assembling an edition of his novels, might also like to buy the remaining copies of *European Acquaintance,* which had reposed in a warehouse for a quarter century.

Unable to convince any other publisher to take up Harpers' offer and lacking sufficient capital to bring out the edition himself, De Forest temporarily let the project lapse. Three years later, however, he wrote to Harpers again, asking them to sell him all the publication rights for seventy-five dollars and not to require him to buy the unsold books. Admitting now that the sales of the standard edition would, at best, only cover costs of production, the aging novelist explained his enthusiasm for such an unprofitable venture. "My only object," he said, "is to leave a small monument for myself. And I must hurry."[17]

This time Harpers cooperated, assigning De Forest copyrights to his three novels, and the writer went looking for a publisher. Assisting in this quest was his old ally, William Dean Howells, who assured him that "the public has been growing toward your kind of work" and that the uniform edition might succeed. Howells wrote to two publishing houses in 1887 and 1890 but to no avail. In 1895 he told De Forest that he still hoped to see the project accomplished and, in a gesture that must have amused and pained De Forest, suggested proposing the standard edition to one more publisher, Harpers.[18]

Though the uniform edition never appeared, De Forest took some satisfaction in publishing two volumes of poems. Paying all the printing costs himself, he produced what he called a "Farewell to the Harp." Half a century earlier, when he had begun his literary career, he had been tickled by the "humorous supposition" that he might be a poet. He had soon recognized, however, that his gifts lay elsewhere, and thereafter he had restricted himself to occasionally placing a poem in a magazine or smuggling it into a novel. Now, though, he gathered up his scattered verses, revised them, and presented them in the ponderous, permanent form of volumes—another monument. The best that can be said of these books is that together they did not cost their author more than a thousand dollars.[19]

The Downing Legends consists of four long narrative poems, two of which are rhymed versions of short stories published in 1869 and 1876. All four pieces recapitulate themes of De Forest's Mugwump stage. The hero of the book is the frontiersman Adam Downing, who "is American 'manifest destiny' in whimsical guise." The whimsy, however, is not always lighthearted. When Downing happens upon Mingo warriors rejoicing over the fresh scalps of "Saxons," he swears

> to stop the breath
> Of every red-skin man and brother
> Who vaunted forth that song of death.

And he does it.[20]

With other Indians, Downing is sometimes gentler, but the result is the same. In the poem "The Last of the Wampanoags," Downing tries to civilize an Indian girl, the last survivor of a "faint and fading" race. She obstinately runs away, however, and Downing must pursue her from the East Coast to the West (symbolic of European expansion). When he catches her at last,

> He seemed to have before his face
> The very last of a fallen race,
> The last of many a tribe and clan,
> The final soul of red-skinned man.

A good-hearted fellow (for all his slaughter of Mingos), Downing cannot harm so pitiful a being; when he raises his hand, it is only to stop a tear form falling down his cheek. But the last Indian becomes a good Indian nevertheless. Refusing to live in a world dominated by palefaces, she sings her death song and drowns herself. Neither Mingo warrior nor Wampanoag maiden can possibly survive.[21]

De Forest has scornful words for humanitarians who might want to rescue the Indian or some other "man and brother" ("The Man and Brother" had been a motto of the antislavery movement). Adam Downing, says De Forest, is a "wondrous wight":

> Far huskier than men we raise
> In these degenerate, mawkish days
> When philanthropic frenzy saves
> Unworthy types from clement graves
> And holds in mischievous subjection
> The law of natural selection.

Social Darwinism was no new theme for De Forest. In one of his Reconstruction articles he had said that he would cheerfully leave the low-down people "to the operation of the great law of natural selection. In other words, 'The Devil take the hindmost.'" Now, in one of his last published works, he was merely restating his belief that "unworthy types" ought to perish.[22]

De Forest's second book of poems, *Medley and Palestina,* was an assortment of verses written at all stages of his career. There were war poems, religious poems, and even a few love poems. The war poems are remarkable because they represent the opposite of everything good in De Forest's fiction. For example, "Campaigning" remembers

> men who battled for a glorious cause
> And died when it was beautiful to die.[23]

Miss Ravenel's Conversion and even *A Lover's Revolt,* in contrast, had shown that death was not beautiful, not even in a glorious cause.

The religious poems in *Medley and Palestina* are interesting mainly because they provide clues to their author's faith. As a younger man, De Forest had repudiated "savory doctrines" of salvation and damnation and had valued Christianity as a humane social code. Charity, he had said in *Witching Times,* was more important than faith or hope. As an old man, he still conceived of religion as essentially a matter of morality, but now he saw some usefulness in savory doctrines. The poem "Despondencies" shows why. A belief in hell, says the poem, long intimidated man into behaving decently. Now, however, hell has been exposed as a superstition, and man, liberated from the threat of eternal torment, is busily creating a hell on earth—hence, despondencies, and also jeremiads. In his religious poems, De Forest acted as a weeping prophet for modern times. Fairly typical of his outbursts was "The City of Destruction," which rhymingly complained of haughty, naughty women and knavish, slavish men. Twenty-five of the poems in *Medley and Palestina* were derived from passages in *Isaiah, Jeremiah, Lamentations,* and *Ezekiel.* As De Forest ruefully gazed about modern America—with its low-bred masses, corrupt politicians, and philistine reading public—he could not help thinking of the backsliding, stiff-necked kingdoms of old.[24]

In these last, unhappy years, as he struggled to erect "a small monument" for himself, De Forest also built one for his family. His new interest in ethnology was accompanied by a curiosity about genealogy. In the 1880s, he employed a Dutch archivist to trace his lineage in France and Holland, and he himself made several trips abroad for that purpose. He sent letters to distant and scarcely known relatives, asking for information about their forebears. By about 1892, he had completed a manuscript on "Jesse de Forest: Founder of New York: His Ancestry, His Emigration, and One Lineage of His Descendants." After eight years of further research, De Forest published (at his own expense) *The De Forests of Avesnes (And of New Netherland): A Huguenot Thread in American Colonial History: 1494 to the Present Time.*[25]

De Forest believed himself the scion of noble stock. In 1888 he was "almost certain" that he was descended from the De Forests of Avesnes, "a family of burgher grandees" who were of noble origin, and he hoped to discover the coat of arms. When a fellow antiquarian and genealogist asserted that Jesse, the first De Forest to come to the New World, was a mere dyer of cloth, J. W. De Forest saw red. "There is not a dyer, or weaver, or laborer of any sort, in the whole tribe," he protested. "They are burghers and burgomasters, . . . they are 'city gentlefolks,' . . . & they probably descended from some cadet of the noble family of Hainaut."[26]

In 1892, though, when he put together the first manuscript version of his family history, De Forest discovered that his revered ancestor Jesse had indeed been a dyer and a draper in Holland; however, he also discovered that this fact was no disgrace. For one thing, it was not uncommon for "patrician breeds" to decline into mercantile or industrial professions. For another, woolen cloth was the staple product of the low countries, so to deal in it was honorable. Moreover, he said, the family were all burghers, and several had held municipal offices—"this at a time when the electorate was very limited, and office was accorded only to the superior class." In *The De Forests of Avesnes,* he reminded the public that, formerly, the wool merchants "constituted a kind of industrial patricianate" and that "the burghers, though not eminent in the social hierarchy, belonged to the classes rather than to the masses."[27]

The dominant figure in both the manuscript and published versions of the family history was Jesse. In 1892 De Forest was convinced that Jesse had led the band of Walloons who settled in New Netherland in 1624; by 1900 he admitted that Jesse may have died in Guiana but asserted that some of his followers migrated to the northern colony after his death. In either case, De Forest believed, his ancestor deserved credit for the founding of New York. Even if Jesse never set foot in New Netherland, he had recruited and inspired the Walloons who went there. When "his" colonists first put spade into the ground, it was "a great historical event":

> The first permanent, cultivating, town-building settlement of New York and Albany had been accomplished by a handful of French-speaking protestants from the Walloon provinces, enrolled by Jesse de Forest of Avesnes. Since then civilized man has not for one day relinquished his hold on the shores of the Hudson.[28]

This great historical event, however, did not easily go down in history. Because many of the Walloons returned to Europe by

1626 and because the rest were overwhelmed by later Dutch and English immigrants, the man responsible for settling New York was forgotten for two and a half centuries. Not until Charles W. Baird published his *History of the Huguenot Emigration to America* (1885) did Americans hear much about Jesse de Forest. As for the hero himself, "Unrecorded he died, perhaps with a bitter sense of having failed in life, as has happened to many whom earth will never forget." J. W. De Forest had sympathy for a man who had fallen into undeserved neglect.[29]

Though Jesse was the cynosure of the family history, more recent progenitors also received attention. John William De Forest respectfully sketched the life of his father, John Hancock, and gave lengthy praise to his uncle David Curtis. One member of the family got rather unfavorable mention—David of Stratford, the man who supposedly rowed a boat up the Housatonic River and founded the Connecticut branch of the clan. Observing that this David was a glazier, De Forest called his career "the humblest one that the family had known since record discloses it as a family."

> I shall be told that a man's a man for aw that; . . . that a republican ought to dance with joy when he finds that one of his ancestors was a plumber or something of the sort. . . . But I must in honesty confess that none of these allegations change my opinions or tranquilize my feelings. The more I think of the matter, the more keenly I regret that my great-great-grandfather was a glazier, and the more I wish that he had had the wit or the luck to be a Patroon, or a governor, or a president of Harvard, or at the least a clergyman.

De Forest made this statement in a humorous tone, but there is no doubt that he earnestly wished that David of Stratford had been a gentleman—like all the rest.[30]

There was something pathetic about De Forest's late, dogged research for his ancestors. He had been steeped in American democracy long enough to know and recite slogans about everyone standing proudly on the base of his individual manhood (as he had phrased it in *Miss Ravenel's Conversion*) rather than boasting of the family tree of which he was a twig. In *Justine's Lovers*, De Forest satirized the pompous Mrs. Starkenburgh, who revered her Dickerman forebears; and in a review of a biography of Admiral David Farragut, he admired the "republican simplicity" that made Farragut indifferent to his noble descent. In a letter to Howells, De Forest mocked "an old gent who has a coat of arms" for being unable to tolerate literary realism.[31]

Even while writing to Howells, however, De Forest himself was looking for the De Forest coat of arms. As he became an "old gent," he could not resist taking a most unrepublican pride in his family. Praising Jesse as Founder of New York and tracing the lineage back to "gentlefolks" in Europe, De Forest found something to brag about—exactly what he needed. A rich man's son who could hardly make ends meet, a novelist whose books were ignored, a lonely man whose own child found him strange and aloof, De Forest acutely needed to reassure himself of his worth. By attributing virtue to the family to which he belonged, he could extract some small measure of self-respect.

In his last years, he needed all the comfort he could get. After suffering for decades from neuralgia and dyspepsia, he was stricken in 1903 with so severe a case of "muscular stiffening" that he was removed to a hospital, where he spent the next three years in unrelieved pain. In 1906, having been rendered practically helpless by accumulated maladies, he was placed in his son's home in New Haven. His mind was unimpaired, but life was torment. Groans from the bedroom filled the house. Finally, on July 17, 1906, he died. The cause of death was heart disease.[32]

He was buried, as were many De Forests, in New Haven's Grove Street Cemetery, the first burial ground in the country systematically to reserve large plots for families so that all the relatives could be laid to rest together. He was not, however, interred near his uncle David or his brother Andrew. Instead he was buried alongside his wife, who reposed among her family, the Shepards. J. W. De Forest, so proud of his ancestors, would spend eternity with his in-laws.

Epilogue

Alexis de Tocqueville toured the United States in 1831 and 1832, when John De Forest was just learning to write. A few years later, the French traveler published two volumes about "Democracy in America," describing the conditions under which De Forest would grow to adulthood, the conditions that would provoke his ideas and words.

One such condition was individualism. Tocqueville said that in democratic nations like the United States, people thought they could be and should be self-reliant. Where social conditions are equal, Tocqueville said, men "owe nothing to any man, they expect nothing from any man; they acquire the habit of always considering themselves as standing alone, and they are apt to imagine that their whole destiny is in their own hands."[1]

J. W. De Forest certainly thought so. Like his fictional Dr. Ravenel, he espoused the principle of "every man standing on his own legs," and as a Union officer in the Reconstruction, he tried to abolish Southerners' propensity to follow the lead or live off the labor of others. When he turned his back on his family's commercial and industrial enterprises and embarked on a career as a writer, he chose to make his own unique way in the world. And he hoped to write the Great American Novel.

Tocqueville, however, had some words of warning. "In America," he reported, "I saw the freest and most enlightened men placed in the happiest circumstances that the world affords; [yet] it seemed to me as if a cloud habitually hung upon their brow. . . ." Americans, he explained, "are forever brooding over advantages they do not possess." Tocqueville attributed this puzzling moroseness to democracy. "When all the privileges of birth and fortune are abolished, when all professions are accessible to all, and a man's own energies may place him at the top of any one of them, an easy and unbounded career seems open to his ambition and he will readily persuade himself that he is born to no common destinies." But such an unlimited future proves an illusion, Tocqueville warns. The freedom that enables a man to rise in society also enables millions of others to rise, and at the top there is not enough room for all. Universal competition is a barrier to success. Democracy thus removes limits from desire but not from achievement, and the result is "that strange melancholy which often haunts the inhabitants of democratic countries in the midst of their abundance."[2]

Melancholy is too tranquil a word for describing J. W. De Forest in his later years. He had performed honorably as an officer in the Civil War and Reconstruction; he had written one superb novel that would earn him a place in literary history, plus enough mediocre novels to earn him a living; yet he got little satisfaction. Believing himself insufficiently appreciated, he damned the reading and nonreading public. He spent his last years assailing the seasons, and he died embittered.

But if, as Tocqueville said, democracy was the fundamental cause of De Forest's unhappiness, De Forest got even. As an old man he repudiated democracy and made an ideal or an idol of gentility. Forsaking his earlier individualism, he conceived of himself not as a unique and solitary atom in the human universe but as a member of the De Forest family. Though he might fall short of his personal goals, though he might never write the Great American Novel, he could take comfort in the fact that he belonged to a great family and "the great Teutonic race." This consolation was not enough to free him completely from his sense of failure; but, small as it was, the solace of family brought relief from the frustration facing even the bravest individual.

Notes

Abbreviations

DCD   David Curtis De Forest, uncle of JWD

DFP   De Forest Family Papers, Manuscripts and Archives Division, Yale University Library, New Haven, Connecticut

JHD   John Hancock De Forest, father of JWD

JWD   John William De Forest

Introduction: "There is not one single great man left in America!" (pp. 1–3)

1. Edmund Wilson, De Forest's most eminent recent critic, calls the novelist "John W." James F. Light, author of the most thorough monograph on the subject, calls him "John William." Most of the original editions of De Forest's novels and stories, however, list their author as "J.W." Abbreviating the first and middle names tilts the emphasis onto the surname, merging the identities of the individual and the family, as in the case of titled aristocrats. The subject of this book seemed to like such an emphasis. His writing was the center of his life, and his pen name indicated what occupied that center: simplicity, austerity, impersonality, family, gentility. Cf. Wilson, *Patriotic Gore: Studies in the Literature of the American Civil War* (New York, 1966), pp. 635–742; Light, *John William De Forest* (New Haven, 1965).

2. J. W. De Forest (henceforth JWD) to George De Forest, Nov. 11, 1852, folder 22, JWD Collection, Beinecke Library, Yale University, New Haven, Connecticut.

3. The word *gentility* is not entirely adequate, for it suggests to some readers a decadence, feebleness, and affectation that I do not wish to imply. *Gentlemanliness* may come closer to the mark, conveying the masculine and muscular sense that JWD intended, but it is so ungainly a word as not to deserve perpetuation. I shall therefore use *gentility* for the quality of being like a gentleman and shall use *genteel* for the corresponding adjective.

Chapter 1: "He is quite a pretty boy and behaves like a gentleman." (pp. 4–15)

1. The most thorough and dependable history of the De Forest family is Emily Johnston de Forest, *A Walloon Family in America,* 2 vols. (Boston, 1914). Also useful is JWD's own *The De Forests of Avesnes* (New Haven, 1900).

2. JWD, *De Forests of Avesnes,* pp. 161–63; William C. Sharpe et al., *Seymour, Past and Present* (Seymour, 1919), pp. 235–37; James H. Croushore, "John William De Forest: A Biographical and Critical Study to the Year 1868" (Ph.D. diss., Yale University, 1943), pp. 5, 10; deed and contracts in folder 109, JWD Collection; William C. Sharpe, *History of Seymour, Connecticut* (Seymour, 1879), pp. 68–69; David Curtis De Forest (henceforth DCD) to Lynch, Zimmerman, May 11, 1821, DCD Letterbook 8, De Forest Family Papers (henceforth DFP), Manuscripts and Archives Division, Yale University.

3. JWD, *De Forests of Avesnes,* pp. 162–63; Anon., *American Ancestry,* vol. 3 (Albany, 1888), p. 185.

4. Will in folder 108, JWD Collection; Sharpe et al., *Seymour,* p. 237; Ezra De Forest to John Hancock De Forest (henceforth JHD), March 7, 1826, folder 65, JWD Collection; Dotha De Forest to Andrew De Forest, March 23, 1827, folder 56, JWD Collection; Dotha to Henry De Forest, Feb. 24, 1827, addition 10, DFP; Andrew De Forest, Diary 2, p. 205, New Haven Colony Historical Society, New Haven, Connecticut.

5. JHD to George and Henry De Forest, Jan. 10, 1826, folder 60, JWD Collection; Dotha De Forest to George and Henry, March 15, 1826, folder 61, JWD Collection.

6. Henry to George, Feb. 16, 1837, photostatic copy of Henry's commission as a missionary, unidentified obituary of Catharine Sergeant De Forest, all in addition 3, DFP; Andrew De Forest, Diary 1, pp. 2–3, 28, and passim; Sharpe et al., *Seymour,* p. 170; unidentified newspaper obituary of George De Forest, dated Sept. 16, 1883, folder 112, JWD Collection.

7. Light, *John William De Forest,* p. 170; Catharine Sergeant De Forest to George Sergeant, Feb. 11, 1847, additional 11, DFP.

8. Andrew to George, March 28, 1836, folder 35, George to Andrew, Oct. [n.d.], 1837, folder 51, Henry to Andrew, Feb. 8, 1837, folder 48, all in JWD Collection; Andrew De Forest, Diary 2, p. 161.

9. JWD, *De Forests of Avesnes,* p. 161; JHD to Andrew, Sept. 3, 1829, folder 56, JHD to George and Henry, March 30, Aug. 21, and Dec. 23, 1826, Jan. 29 and Feb. 7, 1827, folder 60, all in JWD Collection.

10. Sharpe et al., *Seymour,* p. 237; JHD to George and Henry, Dec. 5, 1826, JHD to Carlos De Forest, Feb. 24, 1827, both in folder 60, JWD Collection.

11. George to Andrew, Sept. 12, 1834, folder 41, JWD Collection; Louis E. de Forest, "Chronology for John William De Forest," MS dated 1933, p. 1, folder 111, JWD Collection; Henry to George, Nov. 16, 1835, addition 3, DFP.

12. JWD to Andrew De Forest, Dec. 31, 1832, and April 13, 1833, folder 56, photostat of unidentified obituary of Andrew, folder 112, all in JWD Collection; Andrew De Forest, Diary 1, Dec. 18, 1847, and Jan. 28, 1848, Diaries 1 and 2 passim.

13. DCD to General Boyd, Oct. 24, 1821, DCD Letterbook 8, DFP; DCD to Charles Stewart, April 20, 1808, Letterbook 3, DFP; JWD to Lucretia (Mrs. Andrew) De Forest, April 7, 1850, folder 21, JWD Collection; JWD, *De Forests of Avesnes*, p. 24; Henry De Forest to Andrew De Forest, Jan. 19, 1839, folder 48, JWD Collection.

14. Andrew to George, April 3, 1834, folder 35, JHD to Andrew, Nov. 9, 1838, folder 36, JWD to George, Nov. 11, 1852, folder 22, JWD to Andrew, Dec. 9, 1852, folder 20, all in JWD Collection; Andrew De Forest, Diary 1, pp. 9–10. For an analysis of Whig elitism, see Daniel W. Howe, *The Political Cultural of the American Whigs* (Chicago, 1979), especially pp. 52–53.

15. JWD to Andrew, Dec. 28, 1851, folder 20, JWD Collection; DCD to Mehitable De Forest, Jan. 10, 1802, DCD Journal 2, DFP.

16. Howells, quoted in Edwin H. Cady, *The Gentleman in America* (Syracuse, 1949), p. 187.

17. Andrew De Forest, Diary 1, pp. 11–19; Henry to George, Feb. 16, 1837, addition 3, DFP.

18. JHD to George and Henry, April 6, 1826, folder 60, JWD Collection.

19. JHD to George and Henry, Jan. 8 and Feb. 15, 1826, folder 60, Dotha to Andrew, Aug. 29 [n.y.] and July 31, 1829, folder 61, JHD to Andrew, Feb. 4, 1839, folder 56, all in JWD Collection; Andrew De Forest, Diary 2, p. 225.

20. Andrew De Forest, Diary 2, pp. 197–205, and Diary 1, p. 1; Andrew to George, June 4 and Sept. 11, 1835, folder 35, Henry to Andrew, March 14, 1834, folder 48, Henry to JHD, June 10, 1835, folder 52, JHD to Andrew, Dec. 26, 1838, folder 56, all in JWD Collection.

21. Henry to George, Nov. 16, 1835, addition 3, DFP; Andrew De Forest, Diary 1, p. 1.

22. JHD to George and Henry, Aug. 8, Sept. 7, Sept. 30, and Nov. 24, 1826, folder 60, JWD Collection.

23. JHD to George and Henry, March 9, 1827, folder 60, Dotha to Andrew, July 31, 1829, folder 61; JHD to Andrew, March 1 [sic], 1833, folder 56, George to Andrew, May 4, 1836, folder 41, JWD to Andrew, Oct. 20, 1837, folder 20, all in JWD Collection; JWD to Henry, and Dotha to Henry, both Feb. 24, 1837, addition 10, DFP.

24. George to Andrew, Feb. 10, 1839, folder 41; JHD's will, inventory of estate, and financial memorandum, folder 108, memo of March 11, 1846, folder 103, all in JWD Collection; JWD to Henry, Feb. 27, 1837, addition 10, DFP.

25. Louis E. de Forest, "Chronology," folder 111, p. 1, JWD Collection; JWD to Dotha De Forest, March 11 and July 9, 1846, folder 24, JWD Collection; Catharine Sergeant De Forest to George Sergeant, Feb. 11, 1947, addition 11, DFP.

26. JWD, *Oriental Acquaintance: or, Letters from Syria* (New York, 1856), pp. 80, 92, 94, 99.

27. Ibid., pp. 81–82, 145.

28. Louis E. de Forest, "Chronology," folder 111, p. 1, JWD Collection; inventory of estate dated Jan. 21 and Feb. 2, 1848, folder 110, and financial memorandum dated Nov. 28, 1849, folder 103, both in JWD Collection.

Chapter 2: "I meant to storm the world's attention." (pp. 16–38)

1. JWD to Andrew De Forest, Oct. 20, 1837, folder 20, JWD Collection; JWD, *History of the Indians of Connecticut* (1851; reprint, Hamden, CT, 1964), p. 357; Andrew De Forest, Diary 1, pp. 13–14.

2. JWD to Andrew, July 31, 1848, folder 20, JWD Collection; Mrs. James S. Pitkin (granddaughter of JWD) to James Croushore, Feb. 10, 1943, cited in Croushore, "John William De Forest," p. 77; JWD, *History,* pp. v–vi and passim; Wilcomb Washburn, introduction to JWD's *History,* n.p.

3. George Copway to JWD, June 12, 1851, folder 74, JWD Collection; Washburn, introduction to JWD's *History,* n.p.; JWD, *History,* pp. 96–101, 175, 183–84.

4. JWD, *History,* pp. 28, 29, 38, 43, 253.

5. Ibid., pp. 68, 348–49, 490; Neal Salisbury, *Manitou and Providence: Indians, Europeans, and the Making of New England, 1500–1643* (New York, 1982), pp. 4–5.

6. *New York Times Saturday Review,* Dec. 17, 1898, p. 856; JWD to James H. Trumbull, Jan. 7 and July 27, 1850, quoted in Washburn, introduction to JWD's *History,* n.p.

7. JWD, *History,* p. v.

8. JWD to Andrew, July 27 and 31, 1848, folder 20, JWD to Lucretia (Mrs. Andrew) De Forest, Aug. 28, 1848, folder 21, both in JWD Collection.

9. JWD to Andrew, Dec. 9, 1852, folder 20, JWD Collection; JWD, *Miss Ravenel's Conversion from Secession to Loyalty* (1867; reprint, San Francisco, 1955), pp. 465–66.

10. Ann Douglas, *The Feminization of American Culture* (New York, 1977), pp. 235–38.

11. JWD, *Miss Ravenel's Conversion,* pp. 19, 38–45; JWD, "The Great American Novel," *Nation* 6, no. 132 (Jan. 9, 1868): 28; *New York Tribune,* Feb. 20, 1879, p. 4.

12. JWD to George, June 7, 1852, and July 23, 1850, folder 22, JWD to Andrew, Oct. 20, 1851, folder 20, all in JWD Collection.

13. JWD to William Dean Howells, Feb. 2, 1887, Houghton Library, Harvard University; JWD to Andrew De Forest, Aug. 29, 1851, folder 20, JWD to George De Forest, June 7, 1852, folder 22, both in JWD Collection; JWD, *European Acquaintance: Being Sketches of People in Europe* (New York, 1858), p. 264.

14. JWD to Andrew, Aug. 29, 1851, folder 20, JWD Collection.

15. JWD, *European Acquaintance,* p. 117; JWD to Lucretia De Forest, Oct. 28, 1853, folder 21, JWD Collection; Mrs. Sally Shepard, Diary, Feb. 15–16, 1856, Boltwood Family Papers, Burton Historical Collection, Detroit Public Library; JWD, *Witching Times,* ed. Alfred Appel Jr. (1856–1857; reprint, New Haven, 1967), p. 113; JWD, "The Lauson Tragedy, " reproduced in James B. Durham, "The Complete Short Stories of John William De Forest" (Ph.D. diss., University of Arkansas, 1967), pp. 918–19. In subsequent mentions of JWD's short stories, I shall refer to Durham's useful compendium.

16. For an example of God as moral legislator, see JWD, *Witching Times,* p. 113; for God as comforter, see JWD, *Miss Ravenel's Conversion,* pp. 71–72.

17. JWD, "Two Girls," *Nation* 6, no. 136 (Feb. 6, 1868): 107.

18. JWD, *European Acquaintance*, p. 5; JWD to Cary (Mrs. George) De Forest, April 29, 1851, folder 23, JWD to George, July 23 [1851], folder 22, both in JWD Collection.

19. JWD, *European Acquaintance*, pp. 37–67.

20. Ibid., pp. 67–68, 76–77, 162.

21. *New York Times Saturday Review*, Dec. 17, 1898, p. 856; JWD to Lucretia De Forest, April 7, 1850, folder 21, JWD to Andrew De Forest, Aug. 21, 1852, folder 20, both in JWD Collection.

22. As it turned out, JWD had sufficient material to produce *two* travel books.

23. JWD to Andrew, Dec. 9, 1852, folder 20, JWD to George, Nov. 11, 1852, folder 22, both in JWD Collection.

24. JWD to George, Nov. 11, 1852, folder 22, JWD to Andrew, Dec. 29, 1853, folder 20, both in JWD Collection.

25. Sharpe et al., *Seymour*, p. 237; JHD to George, Dec. 11, 1825, folder 57, JWD Collection; JWD, *The Bloody Chasm* (New York, 1881), p. 165.

26. JWD to Andrew De Forest, Dec. 29, 1853, folder 20, JWD Collection.

27. Croushore, "John William De Forest," p. 131.

28. Gerald F. Shepard, comp., *The Shepard Families of New England*, vol. 1 (New Haven, 1971), pp. 64, 144; *Appletons' Cyclopedia of American Biography*, vol. 5 (New York, 1888), p. 494; JWD, *A Union Officer in the Reconstruction*, ed. James H. Croushore and David M. Potter (New Haven, 1948), p. xvii; Croushore, "John William De Forest," p. 131; Edward R. Hagemann, "J. W. De Forest and the American Scene" (Ph.D. diss., Indiana University, 1954), p. 11 fn.; Sally Shepard, Diary, Feb. 15–18, 1856, Boltwood Family Papers.

29. Gerald Shepard, *Shepard Families*, pp. 145, 287; Sally Shepard, Diary, Feb. 3, 1856, Boltwood Family Papers; Rev. George Shepard, Diary, July 9, 1857, Jan. 21, 24, and 25, 1865, and March 6, 1865, Boltwood Family Papers; Harriet to Aunt [illegible], Sunday, [n.d.], Fanny B. Shepard to Edward Boltwood, Feb. 7, 1859, both in Boltwood Family Papers; Light, *John William De Forest*, p. 40; JWD, *Miss Ravenel's Conversion*, p. 136.

30. Poems in folder 13, JWD Collection; Charles U. Shepard to "Dear Nephew," Nov. 2, 1855, Boltwood Family Papers.

31. JWD to Andrew De Forest, Nov. 9, 1855, folder 20, JWD Collection.

32. JWD, *Oriental Acquaintance*, pp. 4–5; JWD to Andrew, Nov. 9 and 14, 1855, folder 20, JWD Collection.

33. JWD to Cary De Forest, Dec. 16, 1855, folder 23, JWD to Andrew, Nov. 9, 1855, folder 20, both in JWD Collection.

34. JWD to Lucretia De Forest, Dec. 31 [1855], folder 21, JWD Collection.

35. Ibid.; JWD to Cary, Dec. 16, 1855, folder 23, JWD Collection.

36. "Notes made by Dr. L. S. de Forest on the Chronology prepared by Colonel L. E. de Forest," typscript dated December 1933, folder 111, JWD Collection; Croushore, "John William De Forest," p. 140.

37. George Shepard, Diary, Aug. 9 and 17, 1861, and Jan. 24, 1865, Boltwood Family Papers..

38. George Shepard to Lucius M. Boltwood, March 5, 1858, and George Shepard to "Dear sisters," Dec. 6, 1860, Fanny B. Shepard to Edward Boltwood,

Feb. 7, 1859, all in Boltwood Family Papers; "Notes made by Dr. L. S. de Forest," folder 111, JWD Collection.

39. JWD, *Justine's Lovers* (New York, 1878), pp. 34, 37. For the genealogy and history of the Shepards, see Gerald Shepard, *Shepard Families.*

40. Sally Shepard, Diary, March 2, 1856, George Shepard, Diary, Dec. 8, 1856, Jan. 5 and 17, July 30, and Aug. 6–8, 1861, George Shepard to Mrs. L. Boltwood, Jan. 16, 1863, all in Boltwood Family Papers; Fanny B. James to Clara Boltwood, April 5, 1878, Burton Historical Collection, Detroit Public Library.

41. George Shepard, Diary, Sept. 1, 1857, and Feb. 24, 1865, Boltwood Family Papers.

42. JWD, "Two Girls," pp. 107–9. For other polemics against feminine thriftlessness, see JWD's *Union Officer,* p. 94; "Annie Howard," *Hearth and Home* 2, no. 15 (April 9, 1870): 234; *The Wetherel Affair* (New York, 1873), p. 167; *Honest John Vane* (1875; reprint, State College, PA, 1960), pp. 14, 69; and *Playing the Mischief* (1875; reprint, State College, PA, 1961), p. 161.

43. JWD, "Henry Gilbert," in Durham, "The Complete Short Stories," p. 205; untitled, undated MS, folder 8, JWD Collection; JWD, *Bloody Chasm,* p. 266. A more sentimental version of the poem was published in JWD's *Medley and Palestina* (New Haven, 1902), pp. 46–47, under the title "The Lottery Valentine." *Bloody Chasm* and "Lottery Valentine" both were published after Mrs. De Forest was dead.

44. JWD, *Miss Ravenel's Conversion,* p. 372; JWD, *Wetherel Affair,* p. 219.

45. JWD, *Bloody Chasm,* pp. 153–54, 265.

46. George Shepard to Charles U. Boltwood, March 10, 1857, Boltwood Family Papers; George Shepard, Diary, June 27 and July 12, 1857, Boltwood Family Papers.

47. George Shepard, Diary, July 9 and August 27, 1857, and Aug. 13, 1861, Boltwood Family Papers; JWD, "The Baby Exterminator," in Durham, "The Complete Short Stories," pp. 177–99; Louis S. de Forest to Louis E. de Forest, Jan. 4 and Dec. 27, 1933, folder 92, JWD Collection.

48. JWD, *Seacliff or The Mystery of the Westervelts* (Boston, 1859), p. 10; JWD, *A Lover's Revolt* (New York, 1898), p. 347; JWD, "The Hungry Heart," in Durham, "The Complete Short Stories," pp. 1013–39.

49. George Shepard to Charles Boltwood, Dec. 15, 1856, Boltwood Family Papers.

50. JWD, *Seacliff,* pp. 229, 347.

51. Ibid., pp. 41, 255.

52. George Shepard, Diary, Sept. 1, 1857, George Shepard to Lucius M. Boltwood, March 5, 1858, Boltwood Family Papers; Louis E. de Forest to Anne Carabillo, Dec. 21, Folder 116, JWD Collection.

53. George Shepard, Diary, Sept. 1, 1857, Boltwood Family Papers.

54. George Shepard to L. M. Boltwood, Nov. 13, 1859, Boltwood Family Papers.

Chapter 3: "My forte is tittle-tattle concerning living men." (pp. 39–52)

1. JWD, *History of the Indians,* pp. 29, 387.

2. Ibid., p. 387; JWD, *Oriental Acquaintance,* pp. 1–3, 284–85.

3. JWD to Dotha De Forest, March 11, 1846, folder 24, JWD Collection; JWD, *European Acquaintance*, pp. 89–90, 93.

4. JWD, *Witching Times*, pp. 186–87, 220, 311; JWD, "Modern Cats," *Atlantic* 33, no. 200 (June 1874): 737–38; JWD, *Oriental Acquaintance*, p. 29; JWD, *European Acquaintance*, pp. 248, 255; *Galaxy* 14 (October–December 1872), pp. 483–94, 604–17, 764–76; *Galaxy* 15 (January 1873), pp. 42–53.

5. JWD to Andrew De Forest, Dec. 28, 1851, folder 20, JWD Collection. See also JWD, *European Acquaintance*, p. 107.

6. JWD to George De Forest, Nov. 24, 1851, folder 22, JWD Collection; JWD, "Olimpia [sic] Morata," *New Englander* 13, no. 50 (May 1855): 216–34; JWD, *De Forests of Avesnes*, p. vi.

7. JWD, *History of the Indians*, pp. 143–44.

8. Ibid., p. 28; Durham, "The Complete Short Stories," pp. 235, 238; JWD, *European Acquaintance*, p. 159.

9. JWD, *Oriental Acquaintance*, p. 145; JWD to George De Forest, Nov. 24, 1851, folder 22, JWD Collection.

10. JWD, *European Acquaintance*, pp. 93, 186.

11. Ibid., p. 230.

12. JWD, *Seacliff*, pp. 319–20.

13. George B. Forgie, *Patricide in the House Divided: A Psychological Interpretation of Lincoln and His Age* (New York, 1979), pp. 6, 73–74.

14. JWD, *Witching Times*, pp. 48, 210.

15. Ibid., pp. 208–10.

16. JWD, *Oriental Acquaintance*, pp. 24, 32–33.

17. JWD, *History of the Indians*, p. 37.

18. Ibid., pp. 38, 44.

19. JWD, *Seacliff*, p. 341.

20. JWD, *European Acquaintance*, pp. 70, 275; JWD, *Oriental Acquaintance*, pp. 29, 80–81. For a discussion of the debunking of the Orient, see Franklin Walker, *Irreverent Pilgrims: Melville, Browne, and Mark Twain in the Holy Land* (Seattle, 1974).

Chapter 4: "A friend of ours . . . has the craze in his head that he will some day write a great American novel." (pp. 53–72)

1. George Shepard, Diary, Jan. 5 and 17, 1861, Boltwood Family Papers.

2. JWD, "Charleston under Arms," *Atlantic* 7, no. 42 (April 1861): 490, 495.

3. As children, De Forest's son and grandson were told that he was in Europe when the war broke out. He may have been but it is also possible that his descendants or their informants were confused by the fact that Dr. Shepard (without his family) had gone to England in July (before Bull Run) and had returned in October or November. See Louis E. de Forest, "Chronology," folder 111, p. 3, JWD Collection; and George Shepard, Diary, June 23 and July 12, 1861, Boltwood Family Papers.

4. George Shepard, Diary, July 23 and Aug. 11, 1861, Boltwood Family Papers.

5. Fanny U. Boltwood to Lucius Boltwood, Oct. 23, 1861, Mrs. George Shepard, Diary, Nov. 18, 1861, George Shepard to L. Boltwood, Nov. 22, 1861, all in Boltwood Family Papers; *New Haven Daily Morning Journal and Courier* and *Daily Palladium*, Oct. 11, 1861, quoted in Croushore, "John William De Forest," pp. 173–74.

6. JWD, *Miss Ravenel's Conversion*, p. 80; *Journal and Courier,* Nov. 26 and Dec. 9, 1861, quoted in Croushore, "John William De Forest," pp. 174–75.

7. JWD, *A Volunteer's Adventures: A Union Captain's Record of the Civil War,* ed. James H. Croushore (New Haven, 1946), pp. xvii, 31–32, 107; JWD to Andrew De Forest, Sept. 16, 1864, folder 20, JWD Collection.

8. Col. Ledyard Colburn [sic], the namesake but not exactly the model for Capt. Edward Colburne of *Miss Ravenel's Conversion,* was apparently not of high social and economic station. Gov. William A. Buckingham was a Republican who had won reelection by only 541 votes in 1860 and therefore may have offered commissions to Democrats who would support him in future elections. Moreover, as a wartime governor, Buckingham may have been particularly eager for bipartisan support.

9. JWD to Andrew De Forest, July 17 and Sept. 27, 1863, Sept. 16, 1864, all in folder 20, JWD Collection.

10. Harriet De Forest to Andrew De Forest, Aug. 4, 1862, folder 30, JWD Collection.

11. JWD to Andrew De Forest, Sept. 16, 1864, folder 20, JWD Collection; JWD, *Volunteer's Adventures,* p. 51. Also see Carter's arguments against taking a black regiment in JWD, *Miss Ravenel's Conversion,* p. 173.

12. JWD, *Volunteer's Adventures,* passim; Light, *John William De Forest,* pp. 65–70.

13. JWD, *Volunteer's Adventures,* pp. 2, 8, 58, 59, 62, 110, 194, 216.

14. JWD, *European Acquaintance,* pp. 198, 225; JWD, *Volunteer's Adventures,* pp. 77, 230; JWD to Andrew De Forest, July 17 and Nov. 27, 1863, folder 20, JWD Collection.

15. JWD, *Miss Ravenel's Conversion,* p. 62; JWD, "Before the War," *Harper's New Monthly* 32, no. 190 (March 1866): 503. For the crusade against materialism, see William R. Taylor, *Cavalier and Yankee: The Old South and American National Character* (New York, 1961), pp. 334–35; and George M. Fredrickson, *The Inner Civil War: Northern Intellectuals and the Crisis of the Union* (New York, 1965), p. 71.

16. JWD, *Miss Ravenel's Conversion,* pp. 319–20.

17. JWD to Andrew De Forest, Sept. 16, 1864, folder 20, JWD Collection.

18. JWD, *Volunteer's Adventures,* pp. 31–32, 53, 228; JWD, *Miss Ravenel's Conversion,* p. 97; JWD, *Medley and Palestina,* p. ix. In Jeffry D. Wert's *From Winchester to Cedar Creek: The Shenandoah Campaign of 1864* (Carlisle, PA, 1987), JWD is mentioned several times in the text and cited in the bibliography, but not listed in the index.

19. George Shepard, Diary, Jan. 14, 21, and 24, and Feb. 9, 1865, George Shepard to "Dear Brother," March 5, 1865, all in Boltwood Family Papers.

20. George Shepard to "Dear Sister," April 5 and Oct. 5, 1865, both in Boltwood Family Papers; JWD, *Union Officer,* pp. xiv–xv; surgeon's certificate, Jan. 25, 1865, folder 100, JWD Collection.

21. JWD, *Union Officer,* pp. xv–xvii; George Shepard, Diary, Sept. 9, 1866, Boltwood Family Papers. For the motives of Freedmen's Bureau agents, see Martin Abbott, *The Freedmen's Bureau in South Carolina 1865–1872* (Chapel Hill, 1967), p. 23.

22. George Shepard, Diary, Sept. 30, 1866, George Shepard to "Dear Nephew," Jan. 27, 1867, both in Boltwood Family Papers.

23. JWD, *Union Officer,* pp. xxix, 44; U.S. Bureau of the Census, *The Statistics of the Population of the United States, Ninth Census,* vol. 1 (Washington, D.C., 1872), pp. 60–61.

24. JWD, *Union Officer,* pp. 1–12; JWD to Dr. A. D. Long, intendant of Greenville, Dec. 25, 1866, JWD to Bvt. Lt. Col. H. W. Smith, Oct. 31, 1866, both in U.S. Bureau of Refugees, Freedmen, and Abandoned Lands, Record Group 105, National Archives; Abbott, *Freedmen's Bureau,* p. 104.

25. JWD, *Union Officer,* pp. 7, 12; JWD to Solicitor J. P. Reed, Oct. 6, 1866, JWD to Clerk of the Pickens Court, Nov. 23,, 1866, both in U.S. Bureau of Refugees, Freedmen, and Abandoned Lands.

26. U.S. Congress, *Report of the Secretary of War,* Part I, 40th Congress, 3d session (Washington, D.C., 1868), pp. 370–467, passim.

27. The article is reprinted in JWD's *Union Officer,* pp. 112–34, of which pp. 127–29 discuss the Smith case. For more favorable judgments of JWD's performance, see William J. McGill, "The Novelist as Bureaucrat: The Structure of De Forest's *A Union Officer in the Reconstruction,"* in James W. Gargano, ed., *Critical Essays on John William De Forest* (Boston, 1981), pp. 173–81; and Abbott, *Freedmen's Bureau,* pp. 24, 44, 127. A few years later, JWD may have had second thoughts about Frazier's guilt. In the novel *Kate Beaumont* (1872), JWD described a shootout between two South Carolina families, in which a Col. Kershaw is killed accidentally by a hard-drinking member of his own family (p. 372). If JWD did see any similarity between the deaths of Miles Hunnicutt and Col. Kershaw, he left no explicit record of it.

28. Carter may have gotten his charisma and profanity from Philip Sheridan. The fictional colonel's physique and sexual adventurousness, however, do not seem to have been properties of Little Phil. Carter may have gotten his surname from Col. Thomas Carter, who distinguished himself in the Shanandoah campaign as the commander of the Confederate artillery. Cf. Wert, *From Winchester to Cedar Creek,* pp. 93–95, 224.

29. JWD to "My Dear Sir," Dec. 28, 1865, folder 31, contract dated Oct. 27, 1866, folder 101, both in JWD Collection.

30. JWD to Harper and Bros., May 2, 1887, folder 31, JWD Collection.

31. *Atlantic* 20, no. 117 (June 1867): 121; *Harper's Weekly* 21, no. 545 (June 8, 1867): 355; *Nation* 4, no. 103 (June 20, 1867): 491–92; *Harper's New Monthly* 35, no. 207 (Aug. 1867): 401; Light, *John William De Forest,* p. 88.

32. JWD to W. C. Church, March 3, 1867, *Galaxy* Correspondence, New York Public Library; certificate regarding copyright, dated March 9, 1867, in folder 101, JWD Collection.

33. Durham, "Complete Short Stories," p. 426.

34. JWD to Church, Feb. 1 and 17, 1867, JWD to editors of *Galaxy,* March 16 [?] and 24, 1868, and April 28, 1869, all in *Galaxy* Correspondence.

35. JWD to Church, Feb. 1, 1867, *Galaxy* Correspondence; Louis S. de Forest to Louis E. de Forest, Feb. 2, 1936, folder 100, JWD Collection.

36. Abbott, *Freedmen's Bureau*, pp. 20–22, 35; JWD, *Union Officer*, p. 39; George Shepard to Mrs. Boltwood, Dec. 4, 1867, Boltwood Family Papers.

37. JWD *Union Officer*, pp. xviii–xix.

38. JWD, "Great American Novel," p. 27.

Chapter 5: "The democratic North means equality— every man standing on his own legs." (pp. 73–93)

1. JWD, *Miss Ravenel's Conversion*, pp. 465, 471.

2. JWD, *Union Officer*, p. 173.

3. JWD, "The 'High-Toned Gentleman,'" *Nation* 6, no. 141 (March 12, 1868): 207; JWD, *Miss Ravenel's Conversion*, pp. 4, 11.

4. JWD, "'High-Toned Gentleman,'" pp. 207–8.

5. JWD, *Miss Ravenel's Conversion*, p. 460.

6. Ibid., pp. 9, 257, 335, 341.

7. Ibid., pp. 254–55, 305, 341.

8. Ibid., pp. 119, 125, 401–2.

9. JWD, *Union Officer*, pp. 152–58.

10. JWD to Andrew De Forest, Nov. 9, 1855, folder 20, JWD Collection; JWD, *Volunteer's Adventures*, p. 77; JWD, *Bloody Chasm*, p. 45. For an analysis of Northern racism, see Leon Litwack, *North of Slavery: The Negro in the Free States, 1790–1860* (Chicago, 1961).

11. JWD, *Union Officer*, pp. 12, 91, 107, 116, 117, 121, 126; JWD, *Miss Ravenel's Conversion*, p. 237.

12. JWD, *Union Officer*, p. 117. De Forest's belief in the inheritance of acquired characteristics seems to stamp him as a follower of the French naturalist Lamarck; however, in the same series of articles, De Forest repeatedly cites "the law of natural selection" (pp. 131, 158), seemingly following Charles Darwin. When discussing human evolution, De Forest uses whichever theory best suits the argument he is presently constructing.

13. JWD, *Miss Ravenel's Conversion*, p. 460.

14. JWD, *Union Officer*, pp. 109, 135.

15. JWD, *Miss Ravenel's Conversion*, p. 156.

16. JWD, *Union Officer*, pp. 152, 194–95.

17. JWD, *Miss Ravenel's Conversion*, p. 230. For analyses of the nineteenth-century belief in Northern industry and Southern sloth, see Taylor, *Cavalier and Yankee;* and Eric Foner, *Free Soil, Free Labor, Free Men: The Ideology of the Republican Party before the Civil War* (New York, 1970). For a recent argument that the South was indeed more leisurely, see Forrest McDonald and Grady McWhiney, "The South from Self-Sufficiency to Peonage: An Interpretation," *American Historical Review* 85, no. 5 (December 1980): 1085–1118.

18. Abbott, *Freedmen's Bureau*, p. 39; JWD, *Union Officer*, pp. 60–61, 66, 141.

19. JWD to Bvt. Maj. Edward L. Deane, April 30, 1867, JWD to Lt. H. Neide, June 5, 1867, both in U.S. Bureau of Refugees, Freedmen, and Abandoned Lands; JWD, *Union Officer*, pp. 83–90.

20. JWD, *Union Officer,* pp. 99, 189–90.

21. Ibid., pp. 104, 189.

22. JWD, *Miss Ravenel's Conversion,* pp. 50, 64, 233–34.

23. Ibid., pp. 156, 368.

24. Ibid., pp. 20, 149, 205.

25. Ibid., pp. 131–32, 143–44.

26. Ibid., pp. 479–83.

27. For a discussion of De Forest's debt to Bunyan, see Cecil L. Moffitt, "*Miss Ravenel* and *Pilgrim's Progress,*" *College English* 23 (Feb. 1962): 352–57.

28. JWD, *Union Officer,* pp. 175–76.

29. JWD, *Miss Ravenel's Conversion,* pp. 423–24.

30. Ibid., pp. 166–71.

31. Ibid., pp. 32–33, 36, 272, 324.

32. JWD, "Great American Novel," pp. 27–29.

33. *New York Times Saturday Review,* Dec. 17, 1898, p. 856.

34. *Harper's Weekly* 11, no. 545 (June 8, 1867): 355; *Atlantic* 20, no. 117 (July 1867): 121.

35. JWD, *Miss Ravenel's Conversion,* p. 72.

36. JWD to Howells, Jan. 24, 1887, Houghton Library, Harvard University.

Chapter 6: "His business does not keep him, and so he works carelessly at it, or he quits it." (pp. 94–110)

1. Scholars have identified ten novels published by JWD before 1880, but there may have been others. According to a story in the *New York Tribune* of Feb. 20, 1879, p. 4, De Forest had already published sixteen volumes of novels and tales, "several" of which "were written anonymously for a series something like that of Roberts Brothers." Even if his two travel books and one history are counted, that leaves three novels unaccounted for (there is no evidence that he ever published a collection of short stories). If his two novellas (neither of which exceeded twenty-four pages) are counted, there is still a shortage of one. *Justine's Lovers* and *Irene the Missionary* were published anonymously—the former by Harpers and the latter in Roberts Brothers' No Name Series—and they may have been accompanied by others.

2. JWD, "Great American Novel," p. 29.

3. JWD to Editors, Sept. 28, 1869, *Galaxy* Correspondence.

4. JWD, "Oversoul," in Durham, "Complete Short Stories," pp. 855, 894.

5. JWD to F. P. Church, Dec. 29, 1869, *Galaxy* Correspondence.

6. JWD, *Overland* (New York, 1871), pp. 1, 166; Louis E. de Forest to Anne Carabillo, Dec. 21, 1933, folder 116, JWD Collection.

7. JWD, *Overland,* pp. 176, 190.

8. *New Haven Evening Register,* July 18, 1906, p. 1; *New York Times Book Review and Magazine,* Sept. 5, 1920, p. 1; "corrected copy" of *Overland,* folder 10, JWD Collection; Harriet De Forest to F. P. Church, Feb. 17, 1871, and JWD to Editors, May 13 and July 12, 1871, all in *Galaxy* Correspondence.

9. JWD to Howells, May 27, 1871, Houghton Library.

10. JWD, *Kate Beaumont* (1872; reprint; State College, PA, 1963), pp. 422–23; *New York Times Saturday Review,* Dec. 17, 1898, p. 856.

11. JWD, *Kate Beaumont*, p. 284.

12. Ibid., pp. 65, 117, 182, 298, 312.

13. Ibid., pp. 53, 144, 336. Col. Kershaw probably was named in honor of South Carolina's Maj. Gen. Joseph Kershaw, who led a successful charge at Cedar Creek. Cf., JWD, *Volunteer's Adventures*, p. 209; and Wert, *From Winchester to Cedar Creek*, p. 178.

14. JWD, *Wetherel Affair*, pp. 169–70.

15. Ibid., pp. 14, 132.

16. JWD, *Honest John Vane*, pp. 258–59; Philip E. Sullivan, "John William De Forest: A Study of Realism and Romance in Selected Works" (Ph.D. diss., University of Southern California, 1966), pp. 128–29.

17. JWD, *Playing the Mischief*, pp. 43, 93.

18. Ibid., pp. 91, 276–77.

19. Light, *John William De Forest*, p. 153; JWD to William Dean Howells, March 11, 1879, Houghton Library; *New York Post*, May 31, 1878, p. 1.

20. JWD, *Justine's Lovers*, pp. 29–34, 53, 113. The scene with Mrs. Starkenburgh so impressed Edmund Wilson that he quoted it at length in *Patriotic Gore*, pp. 720–28.

21. JWD, *Irene the Missionary* (Boston, 1879); JWD to Howells, March 11, 1879, Houghton Library.

22. James W. Gargano, "John W. De Forest: A Critical Study of His Novels" (Ph.D. diss., Cornell University, 1955), p. 324.

23. JWD, *Bloody Chasm*, pp. 101, 145.

24. JWD, *Wetherel Affair*, p. 12; JWD, *Bloody Chasm*, p. 101; Durham, "Complete Short Stories," p. 1407.

25. *North American Review* 115, no. 237 (Oct. 1872): 366–69; *Nation* 14, no. 351 (March 21, 1872): 190; *Nation* 19, no. 496 (Dec. 31, 1874): 441; *Nation* 21, no. 528 (Aug. 12, 1875): 106; *Atlantic* 34, no. 202 (Aug. 1874): 229; Anne D. Jenovese, "John William De Forest, Realist and Soldier," unfinished diss., University of Pennsylvania, ca. 1934, ch. 7, pp. 1 and 3, in folder 117, JWD Collection; Light, *John William De Forest*, p. 164, James Gargano in "John W. De Forest and the Critics," *American Literary Realism 1870–1910* 4 (Fall 1968): 57–64, demonstrates that many contemporary critics evaluated JWD's work generously and often perceptively.

26. JWD to Harper and Bros., May 2, 1887, folder 31, JWD Collection; JWD, *Wetherel Affair*, pp. 116, 124–25; JWD to Howells, March 11, 1879, Houghton Library.

27. *New York Times*, July 11, 1875, p. 1; JWD, "Crumbs of Travel," *Atlantic Monthly* 38, no. 230 (Dec. 1876): 699, 701; *Nation* 23, no. 587 (Sept. 28, 1876): 196–97; *New York Tribune*, Feb. 20, 1879, p. 4.

28. Louis E. de Forest, "Chronology," folder 111, pp. 3–4, JWD Collection; Light, *John William De Forest*, p. 103; JWD, "Modern Cats," p. 742; Fanny B. James to Clara Boltwood, April 5, 1878, Boltwood Family Papers; Connecticut, probate records for Harriet S. De Forest, Connecticut State Library, Hartford.

29. *New York Times*, Sept. 6, 1880, p. 4; Forrest Wilson, *Crusader in Crinoline: The Life of Harriet Beecher Stowe* (Philadelphia, 1941), p. 619; JWD to T. R. Lounsbury, Jan. 28, 1883, Thomas R. Lounsbury Papers, Yale University Library, New Haven.

30. JWD to William Dean Howells, Sept. 2, 1874, and March 1, 1877, both in Houghton Library; JWD to Daniel Cady Eaton, April 25, 1882, Daniel Cady Eaton Papers, Yale University Library, New Haven.

Chapter 7: "American freemen hate an aristocrat." (pp. 111–130)

1. There is no evidence that JWD joined the Independent Republicans, who deserted James G. Blaine for Grover Cleveland in 1884, and such a move seems unlikely. In the 1870s, JWD had deplored Reconstruction as well as corruption in the Grant administration but had stuck with the Grand Old Party nevertheless.

2. JWD, *Bloody Chasm*, p. 28; JWD, "Annie Howard," p. 218; JWD, *Wetherel Affair*, pp. 95–96; JWD, *Irene the Missionary*, pp. 371–72.

3. JWD, "The Duchesne Estate," in Durham, "Complete Short Stories," p. 654; JWD, "The Colored Member," in Durham, pp. 1122, 1124; JWD, *Playing the Mischief*, p. 61; JWD, *Bloody Chasm*, p. 88. Leo B. Levy, "Naturalism in the Making: De Forest's *Honest John Vane*," in Gargano, *Critical Essays*, p. 140, shows that JWD's use of bestial metaphors reflects his disgust with mankind and democracy.

4. JWD, "Colored Member," Durham, pp. 1121–44; JWD, *Justine's Lovers*, pp. 103–4; *Nation* 23, no. 587 (Sept. 28, 1876): 1196–97.

5. JWD, *Overland*, pp. 21–22; JWD, *Wetherel Affair*, p. 180; JWD, "The Man With a Nose Like an Owl," Durham, pp. 1108–20; JWD, "Father Higgins's Preferment," Durham, pp. 1200–14; *Nation* 14, no. 357 (May 2, 1872): 294.

6. JWD, "The Russians on the Bosphorus," *Atlantic* 41, no. 246 (April 1878): 510–12.

7. JWD, *Overland*, pp. 16, 33, 55; JWD, "Annie Howard," pp. 202, 249, 266, 298; JWD, *Playing the Mischief*, pp. 126–27, 206.

8. JWD, "Della," *Hearth and Home* 2, nos. 7–13 (Feb. 5–March 19, 1870): 105–203 passim.

9. Ibid., pp. 106, 138.

10. JWD, *Wetherel Affair*, p. 164; JWD, "Annie Howard," pp. 266, 347; JWD, *Kate Beaumont*, pp. 186–87, 257; JWD, *Justine's Lovers*, pp. 20, 38, 44, 102; JWD, *Bloody Chasm*, p. 83. JWD's notion of femininity perfectly fits the description given in Barbara Welter, "The Cult of True Womanhood: 1820–1860," *American Quarterly* 18 (Summer 1966): 151–74.

11. JWD, *Seacliff*, p. 349; JWD, *Union Officer*, pp. 139, 152–57.

12. JWD, "Great American Novel," p. 28.

13. JWD, "A Revival of the Papacy," *Galaxy* 14, no. 4 (October 1872): 492; JWD, *Wetherel Affair*, pp. 103, 123.

14. JWD, *Bloody Chasm*, pp. 10, 15, 108–9, 133, 272, 282.

15. JWD, *Seacliff*, pp. 18–19; JWD, *Honest John Vane*, p. 7. For other early satires on parvenus, see JWD's *Oriental Acquaintance*, pp. 96–97, and *Witching Times*, pp. 34–35, 39, 47, 78–80.

16. JWD, *Miss Ravenel's Conversion*, p. 467; JWD, *Overland*, p. 8; JWD, *Kate Beaumont*, p. 391; JWD, *Wetherel Affair*, pp. 36, 56, 221; JWD, *Playing the Mischief*, pp. 113, 122–23; JWD, *Justine's Lovers*, p. 89; JWD, *Irene the Missionary*, pp. 86, 389; JWD, *Bloody Chasm*, pp. 56–57.

17. JWD, "The Lauson Tragedy," in Durham, "Complete Short Stories," pp. 904–5; JWD, *Wetherel Affair,* pp. 19, 44, 148.

18. JWD, *Honest John Vane,* pp. 231–32; JWD, *Playing the Mischief,* pp. 276–77. Far from being of aristocratic lineage, Josie is descended from Goody Umberfield, a seventeenth-century witch.

19. JWD, *Honest John Vane,* pp. 157–58, 175.

20. JWD, *Union Officer,* p. 121; JWD, *Kate Beaumont,* p. 235.

21. JWD, "Russians on the Bosphorus," p. 510; JWD, *Overland,* pp. 37, 128; JWD, "Yesebel," in Durham, "Complete Short Stories," pp. 1388, 1395.

22. JWD, *Wetherel Affair,* pp. 9. 88; JWD, *Playing the Mischief,* p. 386.

23. JWD, *Justine's Lovers,* p. 27. At first glance, this novel seems to refute the notion that "we are the sons of our fathers." Ralph Starkenburgh is an honorable man, but his son Henry breaks his engagement to Justine when she loses her fortune. Henry seems to be living proof that heredity does not matter—until one meets Henry's mother. Mrs. Starkenburgh (née Dickerman) is as cold-hearted as her son and is in fact the source of his egotism.

24. Francis Galton, *Hereditary Genius* (London, 1869), pp. 1, 362. This book was truer to individualism than were JWD's novels of the 1870s. While JWD allowed his heroes and heroines to live off huge inheritances, Galton thought one's own labor should be one's main source of income. Whereas JWD spoke of "the great Teutonic race," Galton deplored the "nonsensical sentiment" that people mistakenly called "the pride of race."

25. JWD, *Wetherel Affair,* pp. 132, 169, 205, 207.

26. Ibid., pp. 115, 140–41.

27. JWD, *Honest John Vane,* pp. 22, 24, 46–47.

28. Ibid., p. 246. In the introduction to the Monument Edition of *Honest John Vane* (1960), Joseph Jay Rubin denies that the book is antidemocratic (pp. 55–56), and he points to JWD's affirmation that the "vast, industrious, decent American public, which wire-pullers usually regard as having no more intelligence or moral principle than one of the forces of nature, showed unmistakably that it possessed much political virtue and some political sense" when it called for an investigation of the Great Subfluvial Tunnel (p. 244 of the original edition). This argument ignores the fact that on p. 252 the "forgiving milk-and-water public" lets Vane off the hook. Edmund Wilson, *Patriotic Gore,* p. 709, is more nearly correct when he says that *Honest John Vane* shows that JWD "was beginning to lose his faith in democracy"—except that JWD had begun even earlier.

29. Henry Adams, *The Education of Henry Adams* (1918; reprint, Boston, 1961), pp. 16, 266; Ari Hoogenboom, "Civil Service Reform and Public Morality," in H. Wayne Morgan, ed., *The Gilded Age,* rev. ed. (Syracuse, 1970), p. 81; William H. Armstrong, *E. L. Godkin: A Biography* (Albany, 1978), pp. 92, 99, 137, 187, 193.

30. Thomas R. Lounsbury, *James Fenimore Cooper* (1882; Boston, 1893), pp. 82, 118–22; Alexis de Tocqueville, *Democracy in America,* vol. 2 (1840; reprint, New York, 1945), pp. 231, 256.

31. Hoogenboom, "Civil Service Reform," p. 85; Henry Adams, *Democracy* (1880; New York, 1968), p. 63.

32. Frederic C. Jaher, "The Boston Brahmins in the Age of Industrial Capitalism," in Jaher, ed., *The Age of Industrialism in America* (New York, 1968),

pp. 194–95, 199–200, 205; Frederic C. Jaher, "Businessman and Gentleman: Nathan and Thomas Gold Appleton," *Explorations in Entrepreneurial History*, 2d ser., 14, no. 1 (Fall 1966): 17–18; William Dean Howells, *The Rise of Silas Lapham* (1885; reprint, New York, 1962), pp. 69–70, 128.

33. Howells, *Rise of Silas Lapham*, p. 128.

34. Hugh Henry Brackenridge, *Modern Chivalry* (1792; reprint, New York, 1937), pp. 7–8, 13; Cady, *Gentleman in America*, p. 125; Stow Persons, *The Decline of American Gentility* (New York, 1973), pp. 69–70, 295; John Higham, *Strangers in the Land: Patterns of American Nativism 1860–1925* (1955; reprint, New York, 1971), pp. 131–57. Of course, not every social scientist considered heredity all-important. The influential R. L. Dugdale concluded that "environment is the ultimate controlling factor in determining careers" (*"The Jukes": A Study in Crime, Pauperism, Disease, and Heredity*, 5th ed. [1877; reprint, New York, 1895], p. 66).

35. JWD, *Playing the Mischief*, p. 57; *Nation* 21, no. 528 (Aug. 12, 1875): 106.

36. JWD, *Justine's Lovers*, pp. 93–94.

37. JWD, *Playing the Mischief*, pp. 208–9.

Chapter 8: "Unrecorded he died, perhaps with a bitter sense of having failed in life, as has happened to many whom earth will never forget." (pp. 131–145)

1. JWD to W. D. Howells, June 24, 1886, Houghton Library; Andrew W. De Forest, Diary 2, p. 221; JWD to Louis S. de Forest, March 4, 1885, quoted in Light, *John William De Forest*, p. 165; JWD to officer in charge of Record and Pension Division, War Dept., Nov. 7, 1897, Louis S. de Forest to Louis E. de Forest, Feb. 2, 1936, and pension certificate, all in folder 100, JWD Collection; Louis E. de Forest, "Chronology," folder 111, p. 4, JWD Collection; Louis S. de Forest, "Notes to the Chronology," folder 111, JWD Collection; *New York Times Saturday Review*, Dec. 17, 1898, p. 856.

2. JWD to Lounsbury, Jan. 28, 1883, Lounsbury Papers; JWD to Howells, Dec. 6, 1886, Houghton Library.

3. William Dean Howells, *The Minister's Charge* (Boston, 1887), p. 368.

4. JWD to Howells, Dec. 6, 1886, Houghton Library.

5. JWD to Thomas Bailey Aldrich, Dec. 26, 1881, Houghton Library; Katherine E. Conway, *On the Sunrise Slope* (New York, 1881), pp. 10, 82.

6. JWD to editor of the *Century*, April 24, 1886, *Century* Collection, Manuscripts and Archives Division, New York Public Library; JWD to Howells, June 24, 1886, Houghton Library.

7. JWD to editor of the *Century*, April 19, 1887, *Century* Collection; JWD to Howells, Sept. 18, 1898, Houghton Library.

8. JWD, *A Lover's Revolt*, pp. 10, 32–33, 49, 170, 276.

9. Ibid., pp. 14, 17, 223; W. D. Howells, "The New Historical Romances," *North American Review* 171, no. 529 (Dec. 1900): 947.

10. JWD, *Lover's Revolt*, pp. 114–15, 293.

11. JWD to Aldrich, Aug. 6, 1883, and JWD to Howells, May 5, 1890, both

in Houghton Library; *New York Times Saturday Review,* Dec. 17, 1898, p. 856. Many of the major works of American literature produced around the turn of the century were not fiction or poetry but history, sociology, psychology, and anthropology: the works of Henry Adams, Thorstein Veblen, William James, and William Graham Sumner, to name a few. De Forest shared these men's interest in "ethnology & other kindred dry matter." Cf., Werner Berthoff, *The Ferment of Realism* (New York, 1965), pp. 150–209.

12. JWD, "The Cradle of the Human Race," *Atlantic* 41, no. 244 (Feb. 1878): 145–57.

13. Isaac Taylor, *The Origins of the Aryans* (London, 1889), pp. 17–20; JWD to Howells, June 17, 1890, Houghton Library.

14. JWD to Howells, May 5, and Sept. 11, 1890, both in Houghton Library; "Editor's Study," *Harper's New Monthly* 81, no. 486 (Nov. 1890): 963.

15. JWD to Howells, Sept. 18, 1898, Houghton Library; *New York Times Saturday Review,* Dec. 17, 1898, p. 856; *Who's Who in America,* vol. 1 (Chicago, 1899), p. 183.

16. JWD, *Volunteer's Adventures,* pp. xii, xviii; JWD, *Union Officer,* pp. xix–xx.

17. Estes and Lauriat to JWD, Feb. 20, 188[4?], Harper and Bros. to JWD, March 1, 1884, both in folder 102, JWD to Harper and Bros., May 2, 1887, folder 31, JWD Collection.

18. Harper and Bros. to JWD, May 14, 1887, folder 102, Howells to JWD, July 29 and Sept. 2, 1887, June 15, 1890, and Jan. 14, 1895, Howells to Levitt [?] June 15, 1890, all in folder 73, JWD Collection.

19. Tuttle, Morehouse and Taylor to JWD, Oct. 4, 1900, March 26, June 15, and Oct. 17, 1901, all folder 102, JWD Collection; JWD to James Brander Matthews, Jan. 24, 1902, Columbia University Library, quoted in Croushore, "John William De Forest," p. 394.

20. JWD, *The Downing Legends: Stories in Rhyme* (New Haven, 1901), pp. v, 73. The poem "The Witch of Shiloh" is a variant of the story "Yesebel" (1876), in Durham, "Complete Short Stories," pp. 1369–1403, while "The Enchanted Voyage" is derived from "A Strange Arrival" (1869), Durham, pp. 626–53.

21. JWD, *Downing Legends,* pp. 89, 111, 114. The title of JWD's poem may have been taken from John Augustus Stone's popular play *Metamora: or The Last of the Wampanoags,* which was first performed in 1829. Metamora, however, was not an Indian girl but King Philip—"the noble sachem of a valiant race—the white man's dread, the Wampanoag's hope"—and Stone's white men were more ruthless and treacherous than Adam Downing. Cf., J. A. Stone, *Metamora; or the Last of the Wampanoags,* in *Metamora & Other Plays,* ed. Eugene R. Page (Princeton, 1941), pp. 1–40.

22. JWD, *Downing Legends,* pp. 161–62; JWD, *Union Officer,* p. 158.

23. JWD, *Medley and Palestina,* p. 8.

24. JWD, *Witching Times,* pp. 113, 336; JWD, *Medley and Palestina,* pp. 50, 167–70.

25. JWD to D. J. Burrell, n.d., addition 11, JWD to Henry S. De Forest, Dec. 11, 1888, and Jan. 28, 1892, addition 4, DFP; George Butler Griffin, memoranda sent to JWD, 1891–1892, folder 115, JWD Collection; "Jesse de Forest:

Founder of New York," undated MS, folder 3, JWD Collection; JWD, *De Forests of Avesnes,* pp. iii–iv.

26. JWD to Eugene De Forest (a nephew), Aug. 14, 1888, folder 27, JWD Collection; JWD to Henry S. De Forest, Dec. 11, 1888, addition 4, JWD to D. J. Burrell, n.d., addition 11, DFP.

27. "Jesse de Forest: Founder of New York," folder 3, pp. 20–22, JWD Collection; JWD, *De Forests of Avesnes,* pp. 24, 37.

28. "Jesse de Forest: Founder of New York," folder 3, pp. 48–51, JWD Collection; JWD, *De Forests of Avesnes,* pp. 76–78.

29. "Jesse de Forest: Founder of New York," folder 3, pp. 48–49, 55, JWD Collection.

30. Ibid., p. 69.

31. JWD, *Miss Ravenel's Conversion,* p. 341; JWD, *Justine's Lovers,* pp. 29–34; JWD, "Farragut," *Atlantic* 45, no. 271 (May 1880): 691; JWD to Howells, Dec. 6, 1886, Houghton Library.

32. Louis E. de Forest, "Chronology," folder 111, p. 4, JWD Collection; Louis S. De Forest to Louis E. de Forest, Feb. 2, 1936, folder 100, JWD Collection; *New Haven Evening Register,* July 18, 1906, p. 1; Light, *John William De Forest,* p. 170.

Epilogue (pp. 146–147)

1. Tocqueville, *Democracy in America,* vol. 2, p. 105.
2. Ibid., pp. 144–47.

References

Manuscript Collections and Government Sources

Boltwood Family Papers. Burton Historical Collection, Detroit Public Library, Detroit, Michigan.

Burton Historical Collection. Detroit Public Library, Detroit, Michigan.

Century Collection. Manuscripts and Archives Division, New York Public Library, New York, New York.

Connecticut. Probate records for Harriet Shepard De Forest. Connecticut State Library, Hartford, Connecticut.

De Forest, Andrew Woodward. Diary. 2 vols. Manuscript Collection, New Haven Colony Historical Society, New Haven, Connecticut.

De Forest Family Papers (DFP). Manuscripts and Archives Division, Yale University Library, New Haven, Connecticut.

De Forest, John William, Collection (JWD Collection). Collection of American Literature, Beinecke Rare Book and Manuscript Library, Yale University, New Haven, Connecticut.

Eaton, Daniel Cady, Papers. Manuscripts and Archives Division, Yale University Library, New Haven, Connecticut.

Galaxy Correspondence. Manuscripts and Archives Division, New York Public Library, New York, New York.

Houghton Library. Harvard University, Cambridge, Massachusetts.

Lounsbury, Thomas R., Papers. Manuscripts and Archives Division, Yale University Library, New Haven, Connecticut.

United States Bureau of the Census. *The Statistics of the Population of the United States, Ninth Census,* vol. 1. Washington, D.C., 1872.

United States Bureau of Refugees, Freedmen, and Abandoned Lands. Selected Endorsements, Letters, and Monthly Reports of J. W. De Forest, Sub-Assistant Commissioner, Greenville, South Carolina, October 1866–December 1867. Record Group 105. National Archives. Microfilm no. 472 in Manuscripts and Archives Division, Yale University Library, New Haven, Connecticut.

United States Congress. *Report of the Secretary of War,* Part I. 40th Congress, 3d session. Washington, D.C.: Government Printing Office, 1868.

Books, Articles, and Dissertations

Abbott, Martin. *The Freedmen's Bureau in South Carolina 1865–1872.* Chapel Hill: University of North Carolina Press, 1967.

Adams, Henry. *Democracy.* 1880. Reprint. New York: Airmont, 1968.

———. *The Education of Henry Adams.* 1918. Reprint. Boston: Houghton Mifflin, 1961.

American Ancestry. Vol. 3. Albany, New York, 1888.

Appleton's Cyclopedia of American Biography. Vol. 5. New York: Appleton, 1888.

Armstrong, William M. *E. L. Godkin: A Biography.* Albany: State University of New York Press, 1978.

Berthoff, Werner. *The Ferment of Realism: American Literature 1884–1919.* New York: Free Press, 1965.

Brackenridge, Hugh Henry. *Modern Chivalry.* 1792. Reprint. New York: American Book, 1937.

Cady, Edwin H. *The Gentleman in America: A Literary Study in American Culture.* Syracuse: Syracuse University Press, 1949.

Conway, Katherine E. *On the Sunrise Slope.* New York: Catholic Publication Society, 1881.

Croushore, James Henry. "John William De Forest: A Biographical and Critical Study to the Year 1868." Ph.D. diss., Yale University, 1943.

De Forest, Emily Johnston. *A Walloon Family in America. Lockwood de Forest and his Forbears 1500–1848. Together with A Voyage to Guiana. Being the Journal of Jesse de Forest and his Colonists 1623–1625.* 2 vols. Boston: Houghton Mifflin, 1914.

De Forest, John William (JWD). "Annie Howard." *Hearth and Home* 2, nos. 13–22 (March 19–May 21, 1870): 201–347 passim.

———. "Before the War." *Harper's New Monthly* 32, no. 190 (March 1866): 503.

———. *The Bloody Chasm.* New York: Appleton, 1881.

———. "Charleston under Arms." *Atlantic Monthly* 7, no. 42 (April 1861): 488–505.

———. "The Complete Short Stories of John William De Forest." Edited with an introduction by James B. Durham. Ph.D. diss., University of Arkansas, 1967.

———. "The Cradle of the Human Race." *Atlantic Monthly* 41, no. 244 (Feb. 1878): 145–57.

———. "Crumbs of Travel." *Atlantic Monthly* 38, no. 230 (Dec. 1876): 696–705.

———. *The De Forests of Avesnes (And of New Netherland): A Huguenot Thread in American Colonial History 1494 to the Present Time.* New Haven: Tuttle, Morehouse and Taylor, 1900.

———. "Della." *Hearth and Home* 2, nos. 7–13 (Feb. 5–March 19, 1870): 105–203 passim.

———. *The Downing Legends: Stories in Rhyme.* New Haven: Tuttle, Morehouse and Taylor, 1901.

———. *European Acquaintance: Being Sketches of People in Europe.* New York: Harper, 1858.

———. "Farragut." *Atlantic Monthly* 45, no. 271 (May 1880): 688–91.

———. "The Great American Novel." *Nation* 6, no. 132 (Jan. 9, 1868): 27–29.

———. "The 'High-Toned Gentleman.'" *Nation* 6, no. 141 (March 12, 1868): 206–8.

———. *History of the Indians of Connecticut: From the Earliest Known Period to*

1850. With an introduction by Wilcolm E. Washburn. 1851. Reprint. Hamden, Connecticut: Shoe String, 1964.

———. *Honest John Vane*. New Haven: Richmond and Patten, 1875.

———. *Honest John Vane*. Monument Edition, with an introduction by Joseph Jay Rubin. State College, Pennsylvania: Bald Eagle, 1960.

———. *Irene the Missionary*. Boston: Roberts, 1879.

———. *Justine's Lovers*. New York: Harper, 1878.

———. *Kate Beaumont*. Monument Edition, with an introduction by Joseph Jay Rubin. 1872. Reprint. State College, Pennsylvania: Bald Eagle, 1963.

———. *A Lover's Revolt*. New York: Longmans, Green, 1898.

———. *Medley and Palestina*. New Haven: Tuttle, Morehouse and Taylor, 1902.

———. *Miss Ravenel's Conversion from Secession to Loyalty*. Edited with an introduction by Gordon S. Haight. 1867. Reprint. San Francisco: Rinehart, 1955.

———. "Modern Cats." *Atlantic Monthly* 33, no. 200 (June 1874): 737–44.

———. "Olimpia [sic] Morata." *New Englander* 13, no. 50 (May 1855): 216–34.

———. *Oriental Acquaintance; or, Letters from Syria*. New York: Dix, Edwards, 1856.

———. *Overland*. New York: Sheldon, 1871.

———. *Playing the Mischief*. Monument Edition, with an introduction by Joseph Jay Rubin. 1875. Reprint. State College, Pennsylvania: Bald Eagle, 1961.

———. "A Revival of the Papacy." *Galaxy* 14, no. 4 (Oct. 1872): 483–94.

———. "The Russians on the Bosphorus." *Atlantic Monthly* 41, no. 246 (April 1878): 503–12.

———. *Seacliff; or The Mystery of the Westervelts*. Boston: Phillips, Sampson, 1859.

———. "Two Girls." *Nation* 6, no. 136 (Feb. 6, 1868): 107–9.

———. *A Union Officer in the Reconstruction*. Edited by James H. Croushore and David M. Potter. New Haven: Yale University Press, 1948.

———. *A Volunteer's Adventures: A Union Captain's Record of the Civil War*. Edited by James H. Croushore. New Haven: Yale University Press, 1946.

———. *The Wetherel Affair*. New York: Sheldon, 1873.

———. *Witching Times*. Edited by Alfred Appel, Jr. 1856–1857. Reprint. New Haven: College and University Press, 1967.

Douglas, Ann. *The Feminization of American Culture*. New York: Knopf, 1977.

Dugdale, R. L. *"The Jukes": A Study in Crime, Pauperism, Disease and Heredity*. 1877. Reprint. New York: Putnam's Sons, 1895.

Durham, James Bascom. "The Complete Short Stories of John William De Forest: Edited, With Notes and a Critical Introduction." Ph.D. diss., University of Arkansas, 1967.

Foner, Eric. *Free Soil, Free Labor, Free Men: The Ideology of the Republican Party Before the Civil War*. New York: Oxford University Press, 1970.

Forgie, George B. *Patricide in the House Divided: A Psychological Interpretation of Lincoln and His Age*. New York: Norton, 1979.

Fredrickson, George M. *The Inner Civil War: Northern Intellectuals and the Crisis of the Union*. New York: Harper and Row, 1965.

Galton, Francis. *Hereditary Genius*. London: Macmillan, 1869.

Gargano, James W., ed. *Critical Essays on John William De Forest*. Boston: G. K. Hall, 1981.

———. "John W. De Forest: A Critical Study of His Novels." Ph.D. diss., Cornell University, 1955.

———. "John W. De Forest and the Critics." *American Literary Realism 1870–1910* 4 (Fall 1968): 57–64.

Hagemann, Edward Robert. "J. W. De Forest and the American Scene: An Analysis of His Life and Novels." Ph.D. diss., Indiana University, 1954.

Higham, John. *Strangers in the Land: Patterns of American Nativism 1860–1925.* 1955. Reprint. New York: Atheneum, 1971.

Hoogenboom, Ari. "Civil Service Reform and Public Morality." In *The Gilded Age,* ed. H. Wayne Morgan, rev. ed., 77–95. Syracuse: Syracuse University Press, 1970.

Howe, Daniel W. *The Political Culture of the American Whigs.* Chicago: University of Chicago Press, 1979.

Howells, William Dean. *The Minister's Charge: or, The Apprenticeship of Lemuel Barker.* Boston: Ticknor, 1887.

———. "The New Historical Romances," *North American Review* 171, no. 529 (Dec. 1900): 947.

———. *The Rise of Silas Lapham.* 1885. Reprint. New York: Collier, 1962.

Jaher, Frederic Cople. "The Boston Brahmins in the Age of Industrial Capitalism." In *The Age of Industrialism in America: Essays in Social Structure and Cultural Values,* ed. F. C. Jaher, 188–262. New York: Free Press, 1968.

———. "Businessman and Gentleman: Nathan and Thomas Gold Appleton—An Exploration in Intergenerational History." *Explorations in Entrepreneurial History* 14, 2d ser., no. 1 (Fall 1966): 17–39.

Jenovese, Anne D. "John William De Forest, Realist and Soldier." Unfinished Ph.D. diss., University of Pennsylvania, ca. 1934. Typescript in John William De Forest Collection.

Levy, Leo. "Naturalism in the Making: De Forest's *Honest John Vane.*" In *Critical Essays on John William De Forest. See* Gargano.

Light, James F. *John William De Forest.* New Haven: College and University Press, 1965.

Litwack, Leon F. *North of Slavery: The Negro in the Free States, 1790–1860.* Chicago: University of Chicago Press, 1961.

Lounsbury, Thomas R. *James Fenimore Cooper.* 1882. Reprint. Boston: Houghton Mifflin, 1893.

McDonald, Forrest, and Grady McWhiney. "The South from Self-Sufficiency to Peonage: An Interpretation." *American Historical Review* 85, no. 5 (Dec. 1980): 1085–1118.

McGill, William J. "The Novelist as Bureaucrat: The Structure of De Forest's *A Union Officer in the Reconstruction.*" In *Critical Essays on John William De Forest. See* Gargano.

Moffitt, Cecil L. "*Miss Ravenel* and *Pilgrim's Progress.*" *College English* 23 (Feb. 1962): 352–57.

Persons, Stow. *The Decline of American Gentility.* New York: Columbia University Press, 1973.

Salisbury, Neal. *Manitou and Providence: Indians, Europeans, and the Making of New England, 1500–1643.* New York: Oxford University Press, 1982.

Sharpe, W. C. *History of Seymour, Connecticut.* Seymour, 1879.

Sharpe, William C., H. A. Campbell, and Frank G. Bassett. *Seymour, Past and Present.* Seymour, 1919.

Shepard, Gerald F., comp. *The Shepard Families of New England.* Vol. 1. New Haven: New Haven Colony Historical Society, 1971.

Stone, John Augustus. *Metamora: or The Last of the Wampanoags.* In *Metamora & Other Plays,* ed. Eugene R. Page, 1–40. Princeton: Princeton University Press, 1941.

Sullivan, Philip E. "John William De Forest: A Study of Realism and Romance in Selected Works." Ph.D. diss., University of Southern California, 1966.

Taylor, Isaac. *The Origins of the Aryans: An Account of the Prehistoric Ethnology and Civilisation of Europe.* London: Walter Scott, 1889.

Taylor, William R. *Cavalier and Yankee: The Old South and American National Character.* New York: George Braziller, 1961.

Tocqueville, Alexis de. *Democracy in America.* Vol. 2. Translated by Henry Reeve, Francis Bowen, and Phillips Bradley. 1840. Reprint. New York: Vintage, 1945.

Walker, Franklin. *Irreverent Pilgrims: Melville, Browne, and Mark Twain in the Holy Land.* Seattle: University of Washington Press, 1974.

Welter, Barbara. "The Cult of True Womanhood: 1820–1860." *American Quarterly* 18 (Summer 1966): 151–74.

Wert, Jeffry D. *From Winchester to Cedar Creek: The Shenandoah Campaign of 1864.* Carlisle, Pennsylvania: South Mountain Press, 1987.

Who's Who in America. Vol. 1. Chicago: Marquis, 1899.

Wilson, Edmund. *Patriotic Gore: Studies in the Literature of the American Civil War.* 1962. Reprint. New York: Oxford University Press, 1966.

Wilson, Forrest. *Crusader in Crinoline: The Life of Harriet Beecher Stowe.* Philadelphia: Lippincott, 1941.

Index

Adams, Brooks, 126, 127
Adams, Henry, 124–26
Aldrich, Thomas Bailey, 136
Allums, Cato, 64, 65, 67, 79
Anglo-Saxons, JWD on: misgivings about, 80; triumph of, 113–14, 135; superiority of, 127; in American Revolution, 135
Aristocracy, JWD on: rejection of, 10, 77; mixed views of, 45–46; admiration of, 102, 118–19
Army, U.S., 55; Twelfth Connecticut Volunteers, 56, 58, 73; effect on JWD, 53, 60, 71
Arnold, Thomas, 9
The *Atlantic*, 54, 67, 69–70, 98, 104, 109, 137

Baxter, Richard, 7, 47
Blacks, JWD on, 67; mixed views of, 28, 78–80; negative depictions of, 112; opposition to "negro misgovernment," 113; argument for segregation, 129
Brackenridge, Hugh Henry, 125, 127
Bristol, Conn., 8
Bull Run (Battle of), 55, 60
Bureau of Refugees, Freedmen, and Abandoned Lands, 63–67, 71, 73, 94, 113
Business, JWD on, 7–8, 14, 60, 117
Butler, Benjamin, 58

Cairo, Ill., 90

Carter, Col. John (*Miss Ravenel's Conversion*), 68, 85–87, 89, 90, 92, 93, 96, 111
Cedar Creek, Va. (Battle of), 54, 59
The *Century*, 134
Charleston, S.C., 27–30, 34, 54–55, 63–64, 66, 69, 108
Chivalrous Southrons, JWD on, 74–76, 81, 87, 88
Civil War, JWD on: as chastening rod, 12–13; as heroic time, 61; as war for democracy, 74, 76
Colburne, Capt. Edward (*Miss Ravenel's Conversion*), 56, 62, 76–77, 84–87, 89–90, 118
Connecticut, 49
Connecticut Historical Society, 17, 19
Conway, Katherine E., 133–34
Cooper, James Fenimore, 90, 125, 127, 132
Crane, Stephen, 93
Crédit Mobilier, 100
Crusaders, 48–50, 60

Darwin, Charles, 122, 158 fn. 12
The Decline of American Gentility (Stow Persons), 163 fn. 34
De Forest, Andrew, 5–9, 11–15, 17, 19–21, 37, 58, 145
De Forest, David of Stratford, 4, 144
De Forest, David Curtis, ix, 4–5, 9, 144, 145

De Forest, Dotha Woodward, 5–7, 12–15; model for "Two Girls," 23, 32

De Forest, Ezra, 5–6

De Forest, George, 5–8, 11–14, 37

De Forest, Harriet Shepard, 54, 62, 71; family history, 26–27, 30–31; model for Miss Ravenel, 27, 68, 85; courtship by JWD, 26–29; marriage, 30–34; separation from JWD, 30–31, 64; illness, 31; spending, 31–32; model for "Two Girls," 32; support for Confederacy, 55; death, 108; burial, 145

De Forest, Henry, 5–8, 11–14, 22, 37

De Forest, Jesse, ix, 4, 142–44

De Forest, John Hancock, 1, 4–8, 12–14, 26, 144

De Forest, John William:

LIFE OF:

—GENERAL: three phases, 3; family history, 4, 142–44; illness, 14, 23–24, 62, 109–10, 131, 145; finances, 14–15, 20–21, 32, 37–38, 70–71, 108, 131; marriage, 29–34, 55, 64, 108; child Louis, 34, 64, 106;

—WHIG PHASE: Whig Party, 9–10; gentility, 10–11; birth and childhood, 11–14; travel to Middle East, 14–15; decision to be a writer, 16, 18–21, 24–26, 28, 36–38; travel to Europe, 21–26; water cure, 23–24, 61; travel to South Carolina, 28–29; rejection of "romance," 50–52;

—REPUBLICAN PHASE: service in U.S. Army, 53, 58–62; vocation as a writer, 53, 63, 71; visit to Charleston, 54–55; recruiting of infantry company, 55–57; difficulty of promotion, 57–58, 61, 63; demobilization, 61; service in Veteran Reserve Corps, 63; service in Freedmen's Bureau, 63–67, 82–83; respect for common people, 74–88; realism, 88–93;

—MUGWUMP PHASE: frustrations as a writer, 95, 97–98, 104–7; travel to Europe, 107, 142; abandonment of literature, 107–9;

withdrawal from society, 109; Mugwumps, 111, 125, 161 fn. 1; alienation from democracy, 111–28; loss of realism, 128–30; living in hotel room, 131; death, 145; burial, 145

WRITINGS OF:

"Annie Howard," 112, 114

"The Baby Exterminator," 34

The Bloody Chasm, 33, 112, 115, 117, 119; analysis of, 104–5

"A Bureau Major's Business and Pleasures," 73

"Charleston under Arms," 54

"Chivalrous and Semi-Chivalrous Southrons," 73

"The Colored Member," 112, 113

"The Complete Short Stories," 152 fn. 15

"The Cradle of the Human Race," 136, 137

"A Daughter of Toil" (unpublished), 134, 136

The De Forests of Avesnes, 142–44

"Della," 114–15

"Doctor Hawley," 62

The Downing Legends, 140–41

"The Duchesne Estate," 112

European Acquaintance, 16, 35, 37, 44, 139

"Father Higgins's Preferment," 113

"The First Time Under Fire," 73

"Forced Marches," 73

"The Great American Novel," 70–73, 90–91, 106, 116, 132

"Henry Gilbert," 32

"The 'High-Toned Gentleman,'" 70, 73

History of the Indians of Connecticut, 16, 44, 47; analysis of, 17–18

Honest John Vane, 99, 106, 120, 126, 128; analysis of, 101–2, 124

"The Hungry Heart," 34

Irene the Missionary, 102, 107, 112, 119; analysis of, 103–4

"The Isle of the Puritans," 47

"Jenny Gridley's Concession," 106, 138

Justine's Lovers, 106, 119, 120, 122, 128–29, 138, 144; analysis of, 102–3

Kate Beaumont, 105, 106, 119, 121, 131, 138; analysis of, 98–99

"The Lauson Tragedy," 22–23, 119

A Lover's Revolt, 34, 137; analysis of, 135–36

"The Low-Down People," 73

"The Man and Brother," 73

"The Man with a Nose Like an Owl," 113

Medley and Palestina, 141–42

Miss Ravenel's Conversion, 3, 43, 56, 69, 73, 74, 76, 81, 94, 97, 107, 111, 118, 119, 124, 138, 144; writing of, 62–63, 67; reviews of, 68; analysis of, 85–87, 89–93

"My Neighbor, the Prophet," 44

Oriental Acquaintance, 16, 26, 29, 35, 42, 44, 104

Overland, 104, 105, 113, 114, 118, 121, 138; analysis of, 96–97

"The Oversoul of Manse Roseburgh," 95–96

Playing the Mischief, 100, 106, 112, 114, 119, 120, 122, 128, 138; analysis of, 102, 129–30

"Port Hudson," 73

"A Report of Outrages," 73

"Rum Creeters is Women," 70

"The Russians on the Bosphorus," 121

Seacliff, 16, 34, 46, 51, 91, 116, 119; analysis of, 35–36

"The Senator" (unpublished), 69

"Sheridan's Battle of Winchester," 73

"Sheridan's Victory of Middletown," 73

"Two Girls," 32, 70

A Volunteer's Adventures, 58, 138

The Wetherel Affair, 99, 105, 107, 112, 113, 115, 117, 119, 123, 128, 138; analysis of, 100–101

Witching Times, 16, 22, 29, 42, 47, 91; analysis of, 35

"Yesebel," 121

De Forest, Lee, ix

De Forest, Louis E., 37

De Forest, Louis S., 34, 64, 106

Democracy, JWD on: superiority to aristocracy, 10; Civil War for, 76, 80–82; "demagogical chaos," 123–24

Democracy (Henry Adams), 124, 126

Divonne, France, 24, 42, 61

Durham, James B., 152 fn. 15

Fame, JWD on: failure to achieve, 61–62, 131; quest for, 137–39

Finney, Charles Grandison, 6

Fisher's Hill, Va. (Battle of), 59

Frazier, Nat, 66–67

Freedmen's Bureau. *See* Bureau of Refugees, Freedmen, and Abandoned Lands.

Gadsden, December, 66

The *Galaxy,* 70, 95, 96, 97, 100

Galton, Francis, 122–23, 162 fn. 24

Gentility: JWD's concern with, 1–3; in De Forest family, 8–11; "high-toned gentleman," 74–76, 86; cult of, 124–28; definition, 149 fn. 3

Godkin, E. L., 125

Graefenberg, Silesia, 23–24, 61

Grant, Ulysses S., 63, 88, 125

Greeley, Horace, 104

Greenough, Horatio, 23

Greenville, S.C., 64, 67, 68, 77, 88

Harper's, 62, 68–70, 73, 92, 113, 134; negotiation over JWD's collected works, 138–39

Hawthorne, Nathaniel, 9, 20, 91

Hayes, Rutherford B., 62, 107

Helen of Troy, 49, 60

Hereditary Genius (Francis Galton), 122

Heroism, JWD on: modern lack of, 1, 40, 46–47, 50; JWD's cultivation of, 24, 72; Civil War's restoration of, 54, 60

Holmes, Oliver Wendell, 91

Howells, William Dean, 126, 131; definition of gentleman, 10; reviews of JWD, 92, 106; correspondence with JWD, 97–98, 104, 107, 132–34, 136, 137, 139

Humphreysville (Seymour), Conn., 5, 13, 15, 17
Hunnicutt, Miles, 65–67

Indians, JWD on: childhood interest in, 16–17; mixed views of, 17–18, 50, 75; negative depictions of, 40, 78, 113
Individualism, JWD on, 10, 42–43, 81–84
Inherited characteristics, JWD on, 79–80, 99, 121–23
Irving, Washington, 20

Jackson, Andrew, 1, 10–11, 88
James, Henry, 20, 106, 128
Jews, JWD on, 42, 113

Kaltwasserkur (cold water cure), 23–24, 59

Larue, Madame (*Miss Ravenel's Conversion*), 43, 68, 85–86, 89–90, 92
Leutze, Wilhelm, 21
Lincoln, Abraham, 10–11, 55, 88
Lounsbury, T. R., 132
"Low-downers" (poor whites), JWD on, 77–78, 80, 88, 116

Manhood, JWD on, 20–22, 59–60, 77
Mather, Cotton, 34, 35
Matthews, Brander, 97
The Minister's Charge (William Dean Howells), 132–33
"Miniver Cheevy" (Edwin Arlington Robinson): allusion to, 48, 147
The Mysteries of Paris (Eugene Sue), 10

The *Nation*, 106, 107, 113, 124, 137
New Haven, Conn., 26, 27, 29, 30, 38, 54, 55, 57, 62, 78, 92, 109, 145
New Orleans, La., 58, 86, 87, 89–90
New York, N.Y., 7, 68, 69, 88, 123, 143–44
Norton, Charles Eliot, 125
Nostalgia, 39, 45, 48, 50–51, 61, 74

Orientals (Middle Eastern), JWD on, 15, 41, 44, 81, 84
The Origin of the Aryans (Isaac Taylor), 136–37

"The Oven Bird" (Robert Frost): allusion to, 1

Palfrey, John Gorham, 18
Pen name, JWD on, 149 fn. 1
Perry, T. S., 106
Persons, Stow, 163 fn. 34
Phillips, Wendell, 62
Pickens County, S.C., 64–67
The Pilgrim's Progress (John Bunyan), 87, 124, 128
Port Hudson, La. (Battle of), 58, 59, 71
Prescott, William H., 126
Priessnitz, Vincenz, 23
Puritans, 7, 35, 43–44, 47–48, 50, 60, 75
Putnam and Griswold, 25

Ravenel, Dr. (*Miss Ravenel's Conversion*), 68, 74, 75, 82, 84, 85, 146
Ravenel, Lillie (*Miss Ravenel's Conversion*), 67, 75, 85–87, 89–90
Realism, JWD on: "poesy" vs. reality, 49; "tittle-tattle," 51–52; in *Miss Ravenel's Conversion*, 91–92; commonplace subjects, 95
Reconstruction, 67, 82, 84, 113
Religion, JWD on: reason and, 5, 14–15, 22–23, 44; piety, 6–7; Protestant ethic, 11, 41–42; Catholicism, 41–44, 107, 118, 133–34; enforcement of morality, 142
The Rise of Silas Lapham (William Dean Howells), 126–27, 133
Romans, 47, 49, 53

Scalawags, 67
Shenandoah Valley campaign, 62
Shepard, Charles, 26–28, 30–31, 37, 54, 55; model for Dr. Ravenel, 68
Shepard, George, 34, 62, 71; criticism of Harriet De Forest, 30–32, 55; criticism of JWD, 37–38
Sheridan, Philip, 62
Slavery, JWD on: "favorable side of," 28–29; fear of uprising, 54–55; criticism of humanitarian reformers, 141
Smith, Bob, 65–67
Social Darwinism, 141
Stowe, Harriet Beecher, 109
Syria, 6, 14–15, 28, 41, 44, 84

Temperance, JWD on, 7, 90
Tocqueville, Alexis de, 125, 146–47; allusion to, 51

Union (Loyal) League, 65–67

Veteran Reserve Corps, 63

Washburn, Wilcomb, 17

Webster, Daniel, 1, 9
Weitzel, Godfrey, 62
Who's Who in America, 137–38
Winchester, Va. (Battle of), 59
Women, JWD on: true womanhood, 33, 115–16; opposition to female equality, 114–16

Yale College, 8, 14, 17, 96, 103

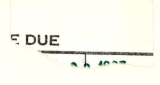